THE HABIT TRIP

The Habit Trip

A Fill-in-the-Blank Journey
to a Life on Purpose

Sarah Hays Coomer

RUNNING PRESS

PHILADELPHIA

Running Press
Hachette Book Group
1290 Avenue of the Americas, New York, NY 10104
www.runningpress.com
@Running_Press

Printed in China

First Edition: on-sale December 2020

Published by Running Press, an imprint of Perseus Books, LLC, a subsidiary of Hachette Book Group, Inc.
The Running Press name and logo is a trademark of the Hachette Book Group.

The Hachette Speakers Bureau provides a wide range of authors for speaking events.
To find out more, go to www.hachettespeakersbureau.com or call (866) 376-6591.

The publisher is not responsible for websites (or their content) that are not owned by the publisher.

Print book cover and interior design by Joshua McDonnell.

Library of Congress Cataloging-in-Publication Data has been applied for.

ISBNs: 978-0-7624-9898-7 (trade paperback), 978-0-7624-9899-4 (ebook)

1010

10 9 8 7 6 5 4 3 2 1

In gratitude for the smallest humans,

who remind us that dogs can talk,

and people can change.

CONTENTS

Introduction xiii

I. The Situation   1

II. The Solution . . . 87

Introduction

In a 1991 address to Columbia University, novelist Salman Rushdie said, "I must cling with all my might to . . . my own soul; must hold on to its mischievous, iconoclastic, out-of-step clown-instincts, no matter how great the storm . . . I've lived in that messy ocean all my life . . . It is the sea by which I was born, and which I carry within me wherever I go."[1]

Or, put more succinctly by the supreme Ms. Dolly Parton, "Find out who you are, and do it on purpose."[2]

As intelligent, functional human beings, we look in all kinds of places for definitive answers about how to improve our lives—how to quit bad habits and build better ones; how to be healthier, more productive versions of ourselves; and how to make time for the people and things we love but neglect. We look for answers everywhere except in the place most likely to steer us in the right direction: our own bodies.

Our bodies offer crucial information that we need to thrive, and this innate knowledge is translated into physical phenomena of all sorts, dispatches from central command. It materializes in the form of vitality, equilibrium, and clarity of mind—or alternatively, muscle tension, indigestion, fatigue, negative body image, or any number of other ailments.

The Habit Trip offers a deliberate method to receive the messages your body is sending and respond in kind with healing reinforcements. It's an actionable antidote for stress and frustration, but this book contains no prescriptions. *You* are the one with all the answers. I have only questions—nestled inside of a whimsical, fill-in-the-blank storybook, in which you are the lead character and the one and only expert. (Plus, for your entertainment, a gaggle of mythical sidekicks and a Ford Pinto.)

What follows is a tribute to your fundamental knowledge of who you are and what you need at any given time to feel whole and healthy. The themes in this book are rooted in intrinsically driven behavioral change, a concept being studied and taught at institutions such as Vanderbilt and Duke Universities, the Mayo Clinic, the California Institute of Integral Studies, and the

National Board for Health and Wellness Coaching. The research these folks are conducting is based on a core, not-so-surprising hypothesis: the experts we traditionally turn to for advice on how to "get healthy" have no idea what is going to *motivate* us to wake up tomorrow and make a different decision than we did yesterday. Only we, as individuals, know the answer to that riddle. It springs from the "mischievous, iconoclastic, out-of-step clown-instincts" we each possess—the brilliant, quirky, and illogical forces that drive us and give our lives meaning.

Our basic needs are universal. We all require safety and sustenance. We're bound together in this curious, asymmetrical journey, and the pleasure—the fun of it—is in the unexpected ways each of us find to keep moving and doing our thing, to keep shaking our tail feathers in all their glory.

This story has nothing to do with what doctors, trainers, or nutritionists say about what you should do to "fix" yourself. It's about you—landing in your body, listening to the messages being sent, and finding ways to respond that feel productive and right.

The Habit Trip is a restorative framework for well-being. It's the utensil tray in your silverware drawer, a tool to help you decide which habits belong—and which are better tossed or swapped out.

With that structure in place, you are liberated to explore what comes next—sustained by tiny doses of daily habits to fill all the needs, scratch all the itches, and fuel all the fires.

"You had the power
all along, my dear."

—Glinda, the Good Witch, *The Wizard of Oz*[3]

PART I

The Situation

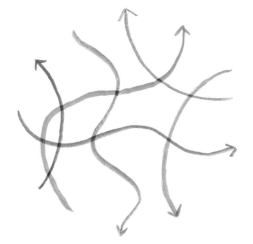

Chapter 1

Which Way Is Up?

Raise your hand if you have no aches and pains, no bad habits, and no stress. If that's you, put down this book and back away. You are superhuman and should make yourself scarce before the rest of us either deify you or imprison you for crimes against humanity. If, on the other hand, you generally feel more like a Tasmanian devil than a Zen monk, settle in.

The Habit Trip is a practice of proactively fortifying your body, heart, and mind with small, life-giving changes—microdoses of solace and structure—in response to the mayhem of daily life. Determine your own dose as you go, and take as needed.

You arrived here today via one road or another. Whether you are an entrepreneur, teacher, designer, parent, farmer, marketing guru, or any other occupation—you have arrived here with some tricks up your sleeve. You've learned a few things, messed up a few, slayed a few, and forgot what you were doing in the first place more than once.

Perhaps you've been circling a roundabout for months or years, unable or unwilling to peel off in a chosen direction. Or perhaps you've just conquered an autobahn of school, career, or family at a face-melting speed and screeched to a halt with your lungs pulsating through your eyeballs. Or maybe you're somewhere in between.

Wherever you're from and wherever you're going, you've developed some habits along the way—ingrained ideas about who you are and ways of interacting with the world that may or may not be helpful. Like them or not, those ideas are familiar. They create a net around your life and keep you feeling safe from the tightrope walk of the unknown. No surprises or challenges. You know exactly how to live within those expectations. Happy or grumpy, impulsive or deliberate, you are who you are, and that's that.

Except not really.

We have more wiggle room than we think.

Enigmatic questions about who we are, how we got that way, and how we react to various circumstances call to mind the age-old nature versus nurture predicament. If you've ever raised a human child, or a feline or canine one, you know that some aspects of their personalities are undeniable. My son has been an observer since the day he was born. He wants to know the lay of the land before he makes any moves. My dog is a turtle, forever in search of a pillow or person to hide under. My best friend is a fire-starter: give her a task and she will build it into a towering inferno. (This is especially useful when the task involves party planning or fundraising.) And I am an animal lover through and through. If you lose track of me at a cocktail party, look under the table. I'm probably on the floor, bedazzled with fur, talking to the resident pets.

Other folks are dyed-in-the-wool competitors, peacemakers, organizers, jokers, artists, or analysts. Whatever your default mode, these instincts are your guideposts, the strengths and values that come to you effortlessly.

But there are also some assumptions that you've painted on throughout the years that aren't so useful, assumptions about how "someone like you" can or cannot be. You slather on a layer of *not-smart-enough*, paint the trim with some *too-fat-for-that*, and touch it all up with healthy splatter of *that's-just-the-way-I-am*.

The paint has dried now, and it's peeling. It's a little itchy actually—and annoying. You're flaking it off with your fingernails, but what you need is a sandblaster—or, if you're feeling moderate, perhaps a nice, wide spackle scraper.

This is your house: your body house. It has lots of secrets to tell you, but it's been awfully dark in there for a good long while. The electricity is flickering; the wiring is functional, but the charge is low. It's hard to see inside. On the outside, you're keeping up appearances but showing signs of wear.

Decoding the parts of our lives that need attention and doing something about them doesn't require an advanced degree in engineering—or a lot of money. We're all different. We all have unique passions and interests, but to show up for them—awake and engaged—every one of us needs the same basic reinforcements. We need rest, nourishment, safety, strong communities, and a reason to get up in the morning. Our minds and bodies are spectacularly functional structures. They're just encased in a little fog, and they need a good, strong wind. This book clears the fog and peels off the drywall, exposing the studs of our lives so we can inspect for termites and rebuild stronger than ever.

By the end of the book, you will have built a personalized platform of behavioral reinforcements for both high- and low-stress periods of life—to stabilize you on the rough patches and build speed and endurance for the straightaways. Once you have the tools, you can apply them over time, whenever you feel like it.

There are ten primary areas of life that impact our health and happiness—Time, Sleep, Food, Fitness, Space, Play, People, Money, Spirit, and Voice—and there are countless ways to enrich each of them. Too many, perhaps, to choose. The options and obstacles can be overwhelming.

Our bodies are the means by which we experience being alive. Everything we encounter is filtered through our five senses, processed by our brains, and translated through our nervous systems. The things we do every day shape our bodies and the circuitry of our brains—and we vastly underestimate the transformative impact of tiny changes that feel like oxygen to the blood when chosen purposefully to fan our individual flames.

When something feels wrong—nothing is working; you want to make a change, but the days are moving too quickly—the impulse is to go big. Start a ten-day fast. Work out five times a week. Quit your job, end your marriage, move to Dubai, and start a tourism company. Raze it all to the ground and start over.

Problem is, you can't start over. You have a physical body to contend with, experiences you have internalized, and ingrained habits that follow wherever you go. The only viable option is to pin your current location and start from there. You are standing nose-to-nose with a greatly improved quality of life, but it's hard to see through that beastly fog.

The Habit Trip maps the topography so you can show up on time for what matters—with a little mischief and a lot of love for yourself and your fellow travelers.

How does your body respond to stress, and how do you alleviate it? What are your triggers and go-to release valves? Which ones are helpful, and which ones leave you feeling like Bill Murray in *Groundhog Day*, rehashing the same negotiations in your head again and again? How do you break the cycle? And what are you doing this for anyway?

You already have the answers. This book will help you find them.

The Orb

Take a moment, if you will, to peek out the window of your house. In the distance, you see something unusual—a crowd of enormous, clear, plastic balls with people inside—rolling free, bumping around indiscriminately, bouncing off rocks, and careening down hills. *What the . . . ? What?* You sit down at your computer to investigate.

According to the Google machine, *orbing* "involves rolling down a steep hill in a gigantic inflatable ball . . . either splashing around inside the ball or flipping literally head over heels."[4] Orbing, otherwise known as sphereing, globe-riding, or zorbing, hit the mainstream in New Zealand in the 1990s.[5] The sport has since spread all over the world to places like Spain, Denmark, and Lewisberry, Pennsylvania, where competitors race downhill at speeds up to 32 miles per hour.

The first time I encountered it, I thought, *Yep. That's pretty much how I feel most days— tumbling head over heels, trying (and failing) to get my balance while the world passes me by.* It's how my coaching clients feel, too. We're scrambling to grab ahold of something, but it's all moving too fast. We can't get our footing long enough to catch our breath, much less maintain a workout plan or start a business . . . or a family . . . or a grassroots revolution.

Orbing is life, y'all. It's a clusterfuck of lawless summer days, unexpected cliffs, and adrenaline. It's a human blender in need of safety rails, and we're all on board whether we like it or not.

But what if we could each build a platform in our respective orbs with some nice, strong handrails to hang on to? We could decorate our orbs with wallpaper, paint, and glitter and allow just the right amount of light to shine through. We could pad them with memory foam or lush cotton pillows. Then we could ride in style with a supportive infrastructure to keep us steady as we free fall.

This is not a fantasy. It's doable. We just need some insight into what's working, what's not, and which reinforcements are most helpful—which habits function like a balm for our inflamed bodies and agitated minds.

Pinning Your Location

As of this writing, I am forty-three years old.

I'm pretty sure that makes me too old to be cool and too young to be wise—but sometimes it's hard to tell reality from bullshit.

I have held the following jobs in my lifetime: CD store clerk, fruit wholesaler, cocktail waitress, bartender, personal assistant, street mime, secretary, actor, HR coordinator, singer/ songwriter, personal trainer, magazine columnist, author, speaker, and health coach.

I have been a daughter, a sister, a friend, a lover, a wife, and a mom.

I have despised my body, sucked in, pinched, and posed.

I have also strengthened my body, hiked, run, stretched, and lifted. I have celebrated my friends, family, and clients. I have traveled some but never enough. I have questioned my judgment and underestimated my value. I have undercharged for my work and overpromised on my time. I have read a million books and written a million words. I have volunteered and rallied. I have coached and trained hundreds of people, listened to their stories, and learned how excruciatingly common our struggles are.

So here—right here and now—I have landed. As I write this, I'm in a pretty good spot. I feel mostly good: safe, and loved by my people. Work is satisfying. I can pay the bills, and my body hurts in only a few intractable ways. But, by the time you read these words, I may be tumbling through the countryside again, holding on for dear life and hoping the support systems I have built can withstand the repetitive blunt force trauma. There is no such thing as standing still. If I sat right here at this desk forevermore, hiding behind this computer screen, in this place that feels so happy and stable, I would grow stale. My muscles would atrophy. My relationships would fail. I would become isolated and afraid to move.

Stability is fleeting, and turmoil doesn't last forever. So the question is, how do we roll with both?

Joseph Campbell wrote in *The Hero with a Thousand Faces*, "A hero ventures forth from the world of common day into a region of supernatural wonder: fabulous forces are there encountered and a decisive victory is won: The hero comes back from this mysterious adventure with the power to bestow boons on his fellow man."[6]

No matter where you have landed or where you came from, you are on your very own hero's journey. Your contribution matters. Your wisdom is real. You have access to all the solutions you could ever need to make your life richer, more fulfilling, and more impactful. I don't have answers for you, but I do have a map, questions, and clues to support you on your way. You will find fill-in-the-blank opportunities throughout this book to help you identify where you are and what comes next.

The world may have turned out to be somewhat less accommodating than you'd hoped when you first woke up as an adult on planet Earth. Leaving your nice, stable house behind to go orbing at the ripe old age of 28 (fill in the blank!) might seem like madness, but you need supplies to keep your house in order. You need tools and fresh paint, lumber for a project out back, and a welcome mat for the front door. If you don't ever move from this place, the roof will begin to leak, the weeds will eat away at your foundation, and the walls will crumble around you.

You have no choice except to keep moving—but not to worry. The hero's journey always leads back home—to your center of gravity, wherever it may be.

Before you go, take a moment to get your bearings, right here in the fog.

There are no wrong answers, only the beginnings of gut instincts, stirrings of the innate knowledge that will tell you what you need and where to go next.

One note of caution: this journey is not intended to conquer the rugged terrain of trauma or abuse. Moving through that kind of territory is a challenge that requires the care and safekeeping of a trained guide. This book is not intended to cure serious substance abuse either. It's not therapy. It's a straightforward process of teasing out frustrating habits—patterns you'd prefer not to repeat (but can't seem to stop), beliefs or ideas you no longer accept—and playing with them to see what else might be possible. Microdoses of well-being are accessible to every one of us—no matter how we got here or how off track we might be.

The voice that matters most in this book is yours, not mine. This is your story, your chance to chart your own course, to explore your motivations and move toward your goals. To do that, you will need to distill your thoughts and—most importantly—write them down.

According to *Forbes* magazine, "A Harvard Business Study found that the 3% of graduates from their MBA program who had their goals written down, ended up earning ten times as much as the other 97% put together, just ten years after graduation."[7] Harvard MBA grads shouldn't get to have all the fun, now should they? We have pens, too. We can benefit from this practice just as well as they can. So:

What brings you here today? Why did you pick up this book?

I want to start to develop good habits and become a better more responsible adult.

In a few words, make a list of personality traits, roles, or stereotypes that have defined who you are—in your own eyes and in the eyes of others.

athlete   funny   quiet
Jock   quirky   shy
rare   full go   stupid
different   full on

Which of those descriptions suit you, and which would you rather not identify with anymore?

Keep
athlete
rare   throw   stupid
different   away   shy
full go   quiet

    Now that we have that out of the way, step outside. Your orb is waiting. It's in the garage, clear as cellophane. It's been there all along. Jump in. Seal it up. Let's go. Throw your weight as hard as you can down the driveway, down the hill, and into the supernatural.

Chapter 2

Ten Areas

of Well-Being

A s the dizzying spin of the orb comes to a rest at the bottom of your driveway, you discover that your house is located at the center of a multidirectional intersection. Stepping onto solid ground, you see roads stretching out in ten different directions.

You steady yourself by leaning on the orb, but it slips out from under you, bobbing away before stopping against a street sign with arrows pointing to each of the ten roads. While you catch your breath, you dig in your backpack in search of a hat to shield you from the brutal persistence of the sun. There isn't a soul in sight. The next phase of this journey is entirely up to you.

At the center of this intersection is your body—the root of your experiences and the messenger that tells you when you've run off the road.

No more spinning out. No more wondering which way is up. No more unidentified flying impulses passing over your head and torpedoing your best efforts before you can grasp where they came from.

In this chapter, you map the landscape. No judgments. No deep dives. Just your initial observations. You're getting the lay of the land and flagging the potholes. In the following sections, you'll have a chance to gut-check each area of well-being and identify challenges you may have by answering two questions per category. This lays the groundwork for the steps you will take in Part II of the book.

Time

As you squint up at the words on the signs, a breeze blows, and the orb rolls slowly toward a road called Time. But this road is not particularly smooth. In fact, it is cluttered with litter and boulders. It looks like there's an old airport in the distance. Between here and there, you see several staircases that seem to lead nowhere at all. There are giant billboards streaming videos about all sorts of things: how to replace a doorknob, viral puppy-cam clips, how to be a better public speaker, how to make a spinach smoothie, instructions for clearing out your hard drive, and—fuck—politics . . . so much politics, so many talking heads. At every crosswalk, there are stacks of papers blowing out of filing cabinets, and the cloud cover over this road is growing. It gets so dim in spots you're concerned you'll lose track of where you're going. The chaos is intriguing, though. You're mesmerized but unsure of how to focus your attention.

This street turns and twists and intersects with every one of the other roads you will explore. *Time* is the most frequent obstacle to change that my clients name. *There simply isn't enough time. I can't carve it out. Every minute of my day is spoken for. I'm stuck at work. I'm stuck with the kids. Everybody wants a piece of me.*

But time is the structure by which we live. If we can build best practices on this road, we set ourselves up for progress in every other part of our lives. Luckily, time comes in small increments. It can be broken down and taken back in pocket-sized, clever little nuggets: one minute, five minutes, fifteen minutes at a time—and in those minutes, we have the power to shape our daily experience.

Chade-Meng Tan is a computer engineer, creator of Google's groundbreaking Search Inside Yourself mindfulness program, and co-chair of the Nobel Peace Prize–nominated One Billion Acts of Peace campaign. In his book *Joy on Demand*, Tan tells a story about an assignment he gave in one of his corporate seminars: At work tomorrow, spend ten seconds at the top of every hour doing a loving-kindness meditation for whomever crosses your path. Simply take a breath, wish that person well, and get back to work.

One of the attendees, a woman named Jane, emailed Tan after doing this exercise. She told him that she dreaded going to work every morning. She hated her job, but the day she had just spent experimenting with this assignment was her "happiest day in seven years."[8] Micro-change: ten seconds per hour. Jane decisively impacted her workday for the better by carving out a total of eighty seconds.

When we talk about time, we are talking about routine—the patterns that structure our days and how minutes are lost or found amid those patterns.

The thought of modifying our routines on a grand scale can be paralyzing, so most of us cover our eyes and plow full speed ahead until we're knocked out by a brick wall we never saw coming. The ways we utilize or surrender our time dictate how much access we have to the people and activities that enrich our lives—and how vulnerable we are to burnout. We know we would feel better, in theory, if we made time for a workout in the morning, took dedicated time away from our phones to accomplish specific daily tasks, or, God forbid, said no to commitments we genuinely do not have time or interest to complete. But in practice, those goals tend to fall apart because they disregard the current, familiar rhythms of our lives. The leap is too far, so we never reach those lofty ambitions—instead, we dig in deeper right where we are, scattered and overburdened. We get behind on all the things and run out of time to reorganize our priorities (or our closets). *Too many pressing matters to attend to!*

Claiming your time in smaller increments, as Jane did, may seem inconsequential at first, but in practice, it can be transformative. Microdoses of time, rightness, levity, breath, movement, and clarity cannot help but change a little something for the better. And when you succeed in following through—with a bit of space here, a breath there, a bath, a walk, or dinner with a friend—you realize, in spite of all the crucial demands on your time, you have the ability to make a palpable difference in your quality of life. That recognition ultimately gives you the agency to address bigger changes, as well.

Time is yours to take, and the scale and substance of those changes are up to you. There will, of course, be parts of your days beyond your control. The joys of adult life do not come without cost, but there are infinitely more opportunities for infusions of pleasure and release than there are lost minutes. What parts of your day are locked in, and which have potential for change?

You'll have a chance to rearrange or reclaim some of that time in Part II. For now—a gut check:

What times of your day feel out of step?

Night — when I don't work - all day.

What is your favorite time of day, and why?

when I get to talk to steph.
game day. - travel day.

Sleep

S elf-help authors, leadership coaches, nutritionists, and other such well-meaning folks will often ask you to consider the course of your day to discover the patterns you fall into—beginning first thing in the morning. It's helpful to get a full-day perspective, for sure, but in my experience, if you start in the a.m., you're behind the eight ball.

Decent sleep makes everything easier, and when we don't get it, we pay a high price. According to Johns Hopkins sleep researcher Patrick Finan, PhD, "Sleep can affect your mood, memory, and health in far-reaching and surprising ways."[9] His research shows that sleep deprivation increases our risk of depression, irritability, forgetfulness, heart disease, dementia, diabetes, the common cold, poor judgment, and good old-fashioned weight gain. It makes us more accident-prone, too. *Great.* One more worry to keep us up at night.

Here's the deal. I have insomnia on a regular basis; I know that agony firsthand. I've endured months when I could barely sleep and have been jacked up by sleeping pills and restless leg syndrome. I get it. You won't find me preaching about how easy it is to fix your sleep woes, but I've also learned a bunch of techniques to handle it when it gets bad, and even better, to prevent the downward spiral in the first place. Most of us can influence our quality of sleep, at least to some degree.

The BBC reports that understanding our circadian rhythms, establishing a "personal, optimal sleep schedule—and [sticking] to it, no matter what"[10] is one of the most important things we can do to sleep better. I'm sure this advice is true, but I find it mildly infuriating. How exactly are we supposed to align our ideal sleep schedules with the realities of stress and obligations? Maybe you're a night person with a small child who wakes up at 5:00 a.m. every day. Maybe you're a morning person who keeps getting called in to work the closing shift. Changing our responsibilities may not be possible, but, one way or another, sleep is imperative. We might not be able to maintain a perfect sleep schedule, but we can definitely make changes for the better.

There are legit clinical sleep problems that can be vastly improved with help from a doctor, but milder problems can be eased by experimenting with behavioral and environmental changes. Stretching before bed, taking a hot bath, shutting off screens at a designated time, getting our thoughts out on paper, wearing an eye mask, using pillows in various ways to prevent pain—all of those have helped me and my clients incrementally over time, but there's no panacea. You probably have other ideas about what might help you—and something is better than nothing. Progress is better than defeat.

How do you spend your evenings as you're winding down? What prevents you from getting to bed at a decent hour? What do you do if you wake up in the middle of the night worrying?

If sleep is an issue, you'll have a chance to explore your options when we get to our action plans: what works, what doesn't, and what's worth trying. (In the meantime, don't shoot the messenger. I'm decoding this puzzle right alongside you.) Getting more sleep isn't so much a decision as a management skill. It's forever in flux.

If sleep is not a problem for you, brilliant. Ignore this section entirely.

This road resembles a bowling lane, smooth and slick down the center—but it's super easy to slip off and fall into the ditch on either side.

What challenges do you have with sleep?
1. _falling asleep_
2. _wake up alot thinking._
3. _staying asleep_

What routines have helped you sleep better in the past, even if just a little?
1. _melatonin - tea, CBD,_
2. _reading - after hot bath_
3. _no caffeine - regular active schedule._

Food

Woo-hoo! It's time for a wonderland of food trucks, fast-food joints, health food stores, farm-to-table restaurants, Cheez Doodles, and other culinary delights. Your cup overfloweth. Your backpack overfloweth! Come to think of it, your stomach probably overfloweth.

Ah, food—we love it; we hate it. It tastes so good and feels so nice. But, oh my God, the ways we misunderstand and manipulate it are driving us batshit bananas.

Food, otherwise known as sustenance or nutrition, is quite literally fuel for living. It's also a way of bringing joy and comfort to others, connecting with family and friends, and celebrating milestones. If you use it for those purposes, you will stroll down this street with blissful abandon. You will take small bites of everything you wish to sample. You'll discover cuisines you haven't encountered before. You'll meet people from all over the world who have stories about how their parents and grandparents prepared feasts for the family. You'll note restaurants you want to revisit and recipes you want to try at home.

If, on the other hand, food more closely resembles a war zone for you, you might find yourself hunched over a bag of doughnuts and a bucket of fish and chips on a curb behind the generators. At least that's where I would have been for most of my twenties and early thirties. You might even find me there now on a particularly bad news day.

How do you feel about food? Is it comforting or stressful? What kind of cravings do you have and when? How does your body feel when you eat various foods? Is cooking therapeutic, aggravating, or somewhere in between? How does food impact your relationships? We'll dive into all of that later in the book, but to get some clarity now, two questions:

What food habits frustrate you?

1. I need to put on weight
2. I need to constantly eat
3. its not enjoying eating what I need to

If you decided to eat something nurturing to ease your hunger before you became ravenous, what foods would you choose?

1. Fish
2. chicken
3. rice.

Fitness

Now that your belly's full, time to move! Grab a bike and let's go! Stand up! Pedal faster! I wanna see some sweat out there!!

Oh wait, your knee hurts? Doc says you need to take it easy? Or maybe you just despise the gym. Yoga's too fluffy. Running is too hard. Weight-lifting is too loud. Swimming destroys your hair.

Totally get it. I get all of it. So many good reasons not to move, so little time. But as I wrote in my last book, *Physical Disobedience*, "Eat for your body; exercise for your mind." Movement isn't about molding your body or making it submit to your fitness fantasies—unless that's for-real your thing and it doesn't make you feel like an uncoordinated sloth.

But for most people, exercise, at its best, is a means of maintaining strength and agility and staying mentally sharp. According to the *Harvard Health Letter*, exercise decreases brain fog by physically "boosting the size of the hippocampus, the part of the brain involved in verbal memory and learning."[11] *Sayonara, fog.* Exercise also decreases depression and anxiety, even when movement increases in increments of only ten or fifteen minutes a day.[12] And—fun fact—fifteen minutes of walking per day has been shown to lower your risk of heart disease *by 33 percent.*[13] Exercise is the peanut butter to sleep's jelly. They fit together like yin and yang.

Those roads just keep on intersecting.

This road feels like one of those race car video games at Chuck E. Cheese. You get to select your vehicle and special enhancements before you hit GO, but once you pull out onto the road, you're flying. If you're super-skilled, you make it to the end flawlessly and take the first-place trophy: You finished the marathon! You got your Pilates certification! You achieved a black belt! But if you're a typical person, you bang up the car a few times before crashing into an oil rig and starting the game all over again: You quit the Couch to 5K. You bailed on bootcamp. You bought one of those "mirror" thingamajigs, but it's creepy so you never turn it on. Time to revisit the token machine.

"Fitness" lost its way somewhere back in the 1980s when it got all tangled up with body image and status. Exercise is a relief for some and a source of endless exasperation for others. For those of us who struggle with it, the problem is usually in how we determine what qualifies as exercise and in the expectations we place on it. Is it for weight loss or vitality? Who even knows anymore? Exercise can increase or decrease our physical pain. It can boost or crush our confidence. No wonder it's fraught with confusion and discomfort for so many people.

Down this road, you get to rediscover fitness for yourself and make it your own. What associations do you have with fitness? Has it been forced on you, or do you love it? Is it important to you—why or why not? How does it impact your life?

If we use our bodies to engage in activities we enjoy, we're onto something supremely valuable. If we force ourselves to perform obligatory drills that make us miserable, we're bound to quit the whole charade in a righteous fit of self-preservation.

Here, you have absolute discretion to never again participate in any physical activity you hate—in exchange for a willingness to find some other way, any other way, to move your body that genuinely feels good. It may take a minute. You have a lot of fitness memes to delete from your memory bank, but "fitness" is painless from here on out.

What does the word *fit* mean to you? How do you define what it looks or feels like?

body composition, I feel fit, I like how I look.

What prevents you from exercising?

1.
2.
3.

Space

T his road is a series of vast tunnels separated by doors, with skylights up above. You step into the first tunnel and find your living room. Do you feel at ease here? Do you like the paint color and the art on the walls? What about the couch cushions? Is the room cluttered with shoes, toys, or dirty dishes? Are there clocks ticking, doors squeaking, or burned-out light bulbs?

As you navigate the physical places where you spend your life, take note of the way each makes you feel. Your living room, bedroom, kitchen, work space, bathroom, outdoor spaces, and car are the backdrop to every day, and they fundamentally influence how pleasurable and functional your life is. Even the place you choose to exercise, or the setup your pet has for eating and sleeping, can impact your mood.

You spend the bulk of your time in these spaces. Not all aspects of your environment can be changed, but many can. On this road, you'll explore manageable ways to supercharge your space.

We all have attachments to possessions and places that might bring up powerful emotions if we try to excavate too deeply. But in our spaces, we can begin to affect change slowly and superficially: uprooting this or that, clearing some clutter from the closet, replacing a broken door handle in the kitchen, sprinkling our homes and offices with tactile luxuries. They don't have to cost much, if anything, to make us feel more grounded.

This is one area where changes can be easier to implement and less emotionally fraught than others, like Food or Fitness. This one isn't a biological imperative (beyond the basic need for shelter, of course), but environment does have a profound effect on our resilience, perspective, and energy levels. This road isn't about spending a bunch of money. It's about cultivating microdoses of comfort in the places we inhabit.

What is your favorite place in your daily environment, and why?

My bedroom - bed. Its my get away space I feel comfrtable and relaxed.

Which of your spaces could use some love?

1. car
2. bedroom
3. Kitchen.

Play

What is play for you, and how often do you take time out for it?

We know that recess is important for kids, and playing improves academic and behavioral outcomes. According to the American Academy of Pediatrics in a policy statement for the Council on School Health, "Recess is a necessary break in the day for optimizing a child's social, emotional, physical, and cognitive development."[14] But somehow parents who rightfully argue at school board meetings in favor of more playtime for their kids don't see (or even consider) the dearth of playtime in their own lives.

Just because we grew up doesn't mean we don't need to take a break, have a laugh, sing a song, bust a move, or stare at the stars.

This road has lots of diversions. It's like Route 66 back in the day. There are lemonade stands, stages with bands playing, craft stations, photography displays, museums, sculpture gardens, pottery wheels, community gardens, movie theaters, knitting workshops, comedy clubs, animal rescues with dogs in need of walking, hospitals with newborns in need of holding, and buildings with group murals being painted.

It's a wonderland. Are you exploring the possibilities or walking down this road with your face buried in your phone?

When and how were the last few times you played? Answers can be big, small, or anywhere in between.

1. ....

2. ....

3. ....

What are the biggest obstacles that get in the way of downtime or play for you?

1. ....

2. ....

3. ....

People

Tread carefully. You're dealing with other humans now.

This road can be blissful, or it can be infuriating. Here, you link arms with the people you see all the time: your partner, kids, best friends, family. Are these people kind? Are they in partnership with you? Do you enjoy them, or are they causing you grief?

As you venture farther down the road, you'll find coworkers; larger circles of friends; folks from school, church, temple, sports leagues, or volunteer groups; and extended family. They are hanging out in familiar places along the way: parks, coffee shops, and friends' houses.

On the horizon, you can see strangers going about their business, and you watch with curiosity. Your current relationships keep you busy, but sometimes you're hungry for new ideas and friendships. You wonder if venturing beyond your inner circle would make life richer and more diverse—or just more hectic. This road offers opportunities to forge new relationships, deepen existing ones, and disengage from destructive ones.

The company we keep is one of the greatest markers of our health and happiness. Recent science suggests that we have something called "mirror neurons" in our brains. Marco Iacoboni is a neuroscientist at UCLA's Brain Mapping Center and author of *Mirroring People: The New Science of How We Connect to Others*. He writes about how these neurons help us perceive and interpret "the actions, intentions, and emotions of other people . . . which in turn leads us to 'simulate' the intentions and emotions associated with those actions. When I see you smiling, my mirror neurons for smiling fire up too . . . I experience immediately and effortlessly (in a milder form, of course) what you are experiencing."[15]

That goes for miserable feelings, too. And food portion sizes. And sleep habits. And ambition, optimism, pessimism, and fitness levels. Between our natural tendencies to mirror those closest to us, the shared expectations of our groups, and peer pressure, we end up looking and acting a whole lot like the people we surround ourselves with.

How are you doing with your people? When and how do you connect with the ones who recharge you? How do you set boundaries with people who deplete your energy? Who do you turn to, or what do you do, when you feel isolated?

The American Psychological Association reports, "According to a 2018 national survey by Cigna, loneliness levels have reached an all-time high, with nearly half of 20,000 U.S. adults reporting they sometimes or always feel alone." It also reports that "a lack of social connection heightens health risks as much as smoking fifteen cigarettes a day or having alcohol use disorder."[16] *Say what now?* Fifteen *cigarettes?*

These statistics tell us two important things. First, if you're lonely, you're in good company. Half of America feels the same way. Second, the people in our lives matter—and we matter to them. By listening, hanging out, and showing up, we are literally saving each other's lives. Two healthy habits we underestimate, at our own peril, are nurturing the relationships that keep us sane—and extricating ourselves from the ones that make us feel measurably worse.

What are some problematic relationships, or lack thereof, in your life? (We'll talk about the supportive, amazing ones soon!)

1. *not having a partner.*
2. *not having alot of true friends present day*
3. *my true friends I hardly see or contact*

Who has set an example for you of what true friendship means? This could be a friendship you have or one you've observed. What did you learn, and how have you carried that example into other relationships?

Steve - cam my arc - Jon, Steph.
learned to be kind and engaging to all

No I haven't.

Money

According to Money.com, "A large analysis published in the journal *Nature Human Behavior* used data from the Gallup World Poll, a survey of more than 1.7 million people from 164 countries, to put a price on optimal emotional well-being." The study found that people's happiness levels rise until their annual income reaches a threshold of about $60,000 to $75,000, and happiness begins dropping off again around $95,000.[17] But how do you put a dollar amount on "optimal emotional well-being"? Depending where you live, $75,000 could be a lot of money or not much at all.

The numbers aren't really the point, but they speak to a fundamental truth: people feel better when they have enough money to cover their basic needs, with a little left over for long-term plans, travel, or pleasure.

Money Street is a mishmash of career, ambition, obligation, indulgence, debt, and financial habits that may or may not serve you in the long run. This road is quieter and more tightly monitored than the others. There are a lot of security cameras around. Most folks don't talk much about their monetary situation, except perhaps to commiserate about how stressful it is. There's a bit of a stench around here, too. It reeks of uncertainty: *Am I earning enough? I'm pretty sure that guy makes more than me.* The pavement is etched with a balance sheet of income and expenses, divergent priorities, retail therapy, instant gratification, discipline, and fear. No matter the status of your bank account, Money Street is a stark reminder of the inequity of birthright, the luck of the draw, and privilege versus hard work. You might feel the need to look away when crossing paths with strangers—unless you are more of a shout-it-from-the-rooftops-and-take-all-of-your-friends-with-you-on-vacation type of person—in which case, cool. You do you.

Money, at its root, is about stress-reduction, security, and freedom. Having enough of it allows us to live without financial strain taking a toll on our health.

We don't always have the option to supplement our education or income. Sometimes survival is the best we can do, but if you have the bandwidth, approaching your financial habits and assumptions proactively can go a long way toward supporting your long-term well-being.

But we're not hunting down random monetary habits, making changes solely for the sake of a number on a bank statement. We're figuring out what can be done to make one or more of those outcomes possible: stress-reduction, security, and freedom.

What is your relationship with money like, and how does it impact your life?

Not toxic. Im in a good family position and job atm
where its not a worry. Does'nt impact me atm.

List any specific money habits or challenges that stress you out.
1. Im too loose with it
2. I don't budget
3. too easy to spend it.

Spirit

Back at the intersection, you regroup. You're almost done with your map, but the last two roads seem irritatingly vague. You're wiped out anyway. The orb is still there, so you could just write off those last roads as unimportant, jump back in, and go for a ride. But as you assess your options, something down Spirit Street catches your attention. You roll your eyes. *Really? Spirit Street? But what is that thing?* You can't tell if it's a moth or a butterfly, or maybe even a hummingbird. You walk closer to inspect it, but it moves away, farther down the street.

As you follow along, you look around. Turns out, this is a mostly pleasant place. There is a lush canopy of trees and a forest with walking trails. There are churches, temples, and mosques dotting the skyline. You find a growing sense of calm as you walk down a shaded path. You feel a little empty—in a good way—tiny but connected. The place is weirdly ethereal. The moth turns out to be a little sprite, a fairy creature. One of thousands. You can't tell if they are angels or devilish little buggers, but they are everywhere. Your curiosity is piqued. The sprites land in the treetops and settle in for the night as the sun begins to set. You watch for a while as the sky cycles through color wheels. You don't have any answers here. In fact, the more time you spend, the more questions you have. Maybe you want to stay forever and soak it in, or maybe you feel disconcerted and anxious. Reluctantly, you turn back to your intersection as the streetlights flicker on.

Spirit can mean whatever you want, but it is rooted in connection, in the stillness that comes when words are no longer necessary. It might mean religious faith or a connection with nature, breathing, meditation, random acts of kindness, or perfecting your guitar solo for when Coldplay comes calling. It's a place, a practice, or a way of being that gets you out of your head.

In what ways is your spirit world exactly as it should be?

....
....
....
....
....

In what ways is it out of sync?

....
....
....
....
....

Voice

The sun has set, and you head down the last road on your map. It seems normal enough: Stop signs and crosswalks. Traffic lanes and medians. All pretty familiar until you come to a dead end in a wide, round, open space. *Is this an outdoor amphitheater or an enormous cul-de-sac?* Hard to say, but at the back there is a giant whiteboard, two stories tall, with unlit floodlights on each of its corners. There's a ladder on wheels that reaches all the way to the top, and a bucket of dry-erase markers in every color of the rainbow. Your name is etched on the top of the board, and at the bottom, there is a light switch with a dimmer. "Turn me on," it reads, in gentle neon.

You look around. Do you feel safe here? The board is yours for the taking. What do you want to write? What do you want to draw? Do you have something to say? If you could communicate any message or draw any image to represent who you are, what you believe, or what matters to you, what would it be? Are you comfortable voicing your opinions? If not, why not? Does something about it feel false? Do you believe your thoughts don't matter? What if someone walked up and saw your work? What if a crowd gathered? Would you flip the board over and write something more presentable?

No need for those answers now. Bottom line: Do you turn on the lights and pick up a marker, or do you walk away? How comfortable are you with owning and expressing your truth?

When, where, or with whom do you feel free to be yourself?

1. Jeff —
2. I feel comfortable now — I did'nt for a long time
3. My team

What people or places make you uncomfortable with your voice?

1. Nightclubs
2. smaller social settings
3. Social scenarios in the team.

When you're done with your whiteboard masterpiece—be it a Pulitzer Prize–worthy manifesto or a giant polar bear cartoon—come back to center. Your orb is waiting for you. It's stable against the street sign. It's not going anywhere. Climb in and curl up for the night. You can evaluate your next destination in the morning.

Chapter 3

What Matters

A s the sun peeks over the horizon, you awake with visions of gridlock dancing in your head. That was a lot to process, a way-too-long list of all the things crowding the forward motion of your life. Now what?

This would be a good time for a morning ritual, you think—if only you had one. Oh well, maybe later.

You step out in the morning light to figure out what to do next. Fog has descended again on your house at the top of the driveway, but from the intersection, you can see pretty well. In the distance, beyond nine of the ten roads, there are imposing mountain ranges. Going in any of those directions would require a lot of trekking uphill, and you're pretty sure you don't have the right shoes for that. But down the road called Voice, past the whiteboard, you see a trailhead. It opens into a field—and that way appears to be downhill.

You decide the orb can stay here at the intersection. Stability seems preferable to speed at the moment. Backpack on, you head out on foot. It's an easy slope, a graceful arc bending over the surface of the earth. Strolling along like the Little Prince on his planet, you put one foot in front of the other: weightless.

This is nice, you think. *I should have done this a long time ago! But where am I going exactly?*

You're headed to your baseline, to figure out What Matters.

In the Game

In 2019, researchers from Northwestern University submitted a study to *Nature Communications*. They wanted to determine the impact of early-career setbacks on subjects' long-term success and whether those rejections signaled a likelihood of future failure. To do this, they examined all of the RO1 Research Project Grant applications ever submitted to the National Institutes of Health. They compared the career trajectories of two groups of junior scientists based on whether they had received grants from their first-ever applications to the NIH. The researchers categorized the two groups as "near misses (individuals who just missed receiving funding) or narrow wins (individuals who just succeeded in getting funded)."[18]

The results were mind-bending.

The researchers found that the scientists classified as "near misses" published *significantly more* hit papers in the first five years . . . and *again* in the five years after that. "The near misses outperformed narrow wins significantly, by a factor of 21%. This performance advantage persisted: We analyzed papers produced in the second five-year window (6–10 years after treatment), uncovering a similar gap."

The upside-down results were especially surprising because the "narrow wins" (the scientists who got their first grants approved) received more funding and notoriety early in their careers. Logically, one would expect that would lead to a significant leg up, but that wasn't the case.

"Over the course of ten years, near misses had fewer initial grants from the NIH and NSF. Yet they ultimately published as many papers and, most surprisingly, produced work that garnered substantially higher impacts than their narrow-win counterparts . . . These results document that, despite an early setback, near misses outperformed narrow wins over the longer run, conditional on remaining active in the NIH system. This finding itself has a striking implication . . . Take two researchers who are seeking to continue their careers in science . . . it is the ones who failed that are more likely to write a high-impact paper in the future."

To extrapolate: Take two human beings who are seeking to keep their shit together and get something done. It is the one who fails *and also remains active in the system* who is more likely to succeed in the future.

The failure itself is a predictor of success, *as long as you stay in the game.*

The question then becomes: When all seems lost, when you've tried everything to change a destructive habit and encountered nothing but failure, how do you stay in the game? *Why* do you stay in the game? If you want to move beyond the challenges you identified in your Ten Areas of Well-Being, you'll need to know why you're making the effort. What's the point? What are you going to do with your newfound momentum? You want to make changes, but what for?

There is no point (and no sustainable motivation) without a purpose.

Something matters to you. Something stokes your fire. Otherwise, you would crawl into bed with a stack of pizzas, a gallon of soda (or wine, depending on your preference), the collected works of Samantha Irby, Joan Didion, and David Sedaris, and all 667 episodes of *The Simpsons*. You'd be all set, right there in your crumbling house, with sustenance, shelter, and diversion. If that's all you needed, you wouldn't bother getting out of bed.

Something is driving you to get up and be proactive. Sustaining your bank account is necessary for survival, of course, but—setting aside how much you may love or hate work or school—some internal compass is steering the decisions you make each day about where, how, and with whom to spend your time and energy. Some obstinate thirst propels your decision-making at every crossroad. It matters to you, and it matters a lot.

What Matters is a constitutional instinct, your true north. It lets you know which choice is right and where you belong in this cacophony of human existence. It's a magnet that pulls you forward, whether you're aware of it or not, and it is relentless. In motivational speak, they call these forces your values. You can also think of them as principles, catalysts, or inspiration. Whatever you call them, they are powerful, visceral influences, and once you know what yours are, they will guide you. They'll hold you up.

I think of them like a stack of sugar packets under a table leg at your favorite diner. They stabilize you when you begin to wobble so you can eat your fries in peace.

Pivot Points

S taying in the game is no fun if you're in the wrong game. Showing up for a job or living in a relationship that goes against your values can be soul-crushing. But when you know What Matters, the Ten Areas become less complicated to navigate. It gets easier to determine when changes, large or small, are warranted.

In 2019, NPR correspondent Yuki Noguchi reported that hospitals in sparsely populated counties all over the country are closing due to bankruptcy and a lack of medical staff willing to forgo higher-paying jobs available in bigger cities.[19] To save the hospitals, administrators in these counties are building recruiting campaigns around the personal values of physicians and nurses they are hoping to attract. They're looking for people who will move in and stick around not in spite of the location, but *because* of it.

A mentor advised one administrator in Kansas, "Go with them and see what motivates them; see why they would want to go there." In doing so, he "found success targeting people motivated by mission over money: 'A person that is driven toward the relief of human suffering and the pursuit of justice and equity.'" The medical professionals who take the leap in Kansas are able to provide care in areas that "have more in common with rural Zimbabwe than . . . with Boston, Mass." Without them, people in these counties would have nowhere to turn, and filling that need is of primary importance to a specific population of doctors. The Kansas hospital provides those same mission-driven doctors ten weeks of paid sabbatical every year to allow them to work overseas.

Another hospital, in a "frontier area" in central Idaho, looks for doctors who love exploring the outdoors, or older, semi-retired physicians who are interested in working part time. "You like mountain climbing, we're gonna go mountain climbing," says the hospital CEO.

Executives in these rural counties have been able to turn their facilities around by appealing to the values of the people they want to bring into their communities. When they recruit the right folks, everybody wins.

What would make someone want to pick up mid-career and relocate to a remote outpost? Plenty of things: The lure of the wilderness. A desire to make a difference. A quieter, less chaotic life. Traffic fatigue. Fewer expenses. Paid time off for purpose-driven missions. These incentives certainly won't appeal to everyone, but they attract the right people, the ones ready to pivot to satisfy their core values.

To figure out What Matters to you, start by listing the most impactful turning points in your life, the times you actively chose to pivot.

Have you ever made a big decision to move to a new town or go to a new school?

Did you decide to get married, break up with a partner, quit your job, start a business, or have kids?

Did you part ways with an old friend or embark on an unexpected adventure with a new one?

Did you commit to a major project or cause that grew to eclipse other parts of your life?

Whether or not those choices worked out like you'd hoped, when and how did you decide to take a leap?

What big changes did you make and when?

1. broke with a partner

2. Started a business

3. Moved countries for work

4. Starting a new relationship with long distance

5. deny aws rughy and leave.

As each of those decisions crystallized, what aspects of your life felt misaligned or stunted? In other words, what were you moving *away* from?

I'm not talking about logistics such as *I wasn't earning enough money* or *My ex was obnoxious.* I'm talking about the passions or belief systems you hold dear that were being denied, frustrated, or ignored. Were you cramped? Disorganized? Misunderstood, suffocated, overwhelmed, or under-stimulated? What limitations could you not abide any longer?

For each pivot point, what were you escaping?

1. under-stimulated and it was a mundane easy life.

2. again boring and unfulfilled so I started a business

3. Wanted more money - new adventure while I'm still able to play

4. New stimulation, new and exciting times,

5.

I guess I did know something didn't feel right back then, you think. *And I did something about it, too! This decision worked out. That other one didn't—and it all brought me here to this verdant little stroll. I guess I'm pretty good at knowing what I don't want. But what do I want?*

Excellent question, Grasshopper!

It's easy to get perspective on the past; hindsight is 20/20. You have a pretty good idea now of what you were moving away from, so what were you moving *toward*? What were you aching for? *Why* did you want to earn more money, leave a bad relationship behind, or get a degree? Did you want stability? Or something else, like adventure? Or respect?

Circle back to those pivot points one last time, and use the following list, Reasons for Doing All the Things, to consider What Matters to you. Mark it up to your heart's desire. Start by crossing out the words that are definitely *not* driving you. Then try using symbols (stars, circles, dashes, happy faces) to indicate which words ring true and which ones feel plausible but you aren't totally sure. Use a color code system if you want. Add new words if I forgot some. (If the options here don't quite resonate, you can find more online by searching for lists of "core values" or "personal values.")

Make this list your own. And don't go highlighting "humility" or "responsibility" just because you think that's what you "should" be striving for. If you're overwhelmed by the options, before diving in, read through the end of the chapter for more examples of how values can function in real life.

This word game is only useful if you level with yourself about what gets you excited, with an unstoppable, "no holding me back" impulse—or what gets you pissed off when you're stifled by circumstances beyond your control. There are no right or wrong answers, only true and false ones. When you stray into the false ones, you can feel them eat away at your equilibrium. The true ones draw you in like honeysuckle on a vine.

These questions are not particularly easy. The values that motivate you can be opaque at first, but they tend to come clear like a sorcerer's stone, offering a guiding light in the fog whenever you're faced with a decision to pivot or simply to try something new.

The bottom of the hill is approaching. The grass is soft under your feet. What do you find there? What makes you the "you-est" you: What Matters?

Reasons for Doing All the Things

Accuracy ~~Accuracy~~

Achievement ✓✓

Adventure ✓

Ambition ✓✓

~~Appearance~~

~~Assertiveness~~

~~Autonomy~~

Balance ✓✓

~~Beauty~~

~~Belonging~~

Challenge ✓

Clarity ✓✓

Community ✓

~~Compassion~~

Competition ✓✓

Connection ✓✓

~~Consistency~~

~~Contentment~~

Contribution ✓

~~Creativity~~

~~Curiosity~~

Dependability ✓✓

Determination ✓✓

~~Devotion~~

Discipline ✓✓

~~Education~~

Empathy ✓

~~Equality~~

Excellence ✓✓

Excitement ✓

~~Expertise~~

Exploration ✓

~~Fairness~~

~~Faith~~

Family ✓✓

Fitness ✓✓

Focus

Freedom ✓✓

Fun ✓✓

~~Generosity~~

Giving ✓

~~Goodness~~

~~Grace~~

Gratitude ✓

Growth ✓✓

Happiness ✓✓

Hard work ✓✓

~~Harmony~~

Health ✓✓

Honesty ✓

Honor ✓✓

~~Humility~~

Independence ✓✓   Peace ✓✓   Security ✓   Support ✓✓

~~Intelligence~~   ~~Perfection~~   Self-actualization ✓   ~~Teamwork~~

~~Intuition~~   Pleasure ✓✓   ~~Self-expression~~   Thoughtfulness ✓

Joy ✓✓   Positivity ✓   Self-reliance ✓✓   ~~Tradition~~

~~Justice~~   ~~Practicality~~   ~~Service~~   Trustworthiness ✓✓

Kindness ✓   ~~Precision~~   ~~Simplicity~~   ~~Truth~~

Leadership ✓   Preparedness ✓✓   ~~Speed~~   Uniqueness ✓✓

Legacy ✓✓   Professionalism   Spontaneity ✓   ~~Unity~~

Love ✓✓   ~~Purity~~   ~~Stability~~   ~~Usefulness~~

Loyalty ✓✓   Reliability ✓✓   ~~Status~~   Vision ✓

~~Mastery~~   ~~Resourcefulness~~ ✓   Strength ✓   ~~Vitality~~

Open-mindedness   Respect ✓✓   Structure ✓✓

~~Originality~~   Responsibility ✓   Success

Sabotage and Denial:
Values in Action

I was irritated the first time I encountered a list like this. *Don't fence me in, man. I can't be pigeonholed. I'm a bird in flight. Just when you think you know where to find me, I've gone the other way.*

But when I step back with just a smidge of self-awareness, I recognize that this specific response, my resistance, in and of itself, proves the point. I don't like labels. I don't like boxes. I want my freedom. **Autonomy** is a driving force at the center of every decision I make. I ache for it. Try to take it from me, and I'm out. The quickest way to drive me away is to tell me that I'm supposed to fit into your paradigm of what a "personal trainer" looks like, how a "mom" behaves, or what being an "author" or a "good girl" means. Beyond being generous and considerate of others, tell me who I'm supposed to be or what I'm supposed to do, and I'll tell you to peace out. *Smell you later. I don't have time for that.*

However, as a health coach, I've seen countless examples of my clients repeating patterns, longing for something different, and struggling to find the motivation they need . . . until they identify their values. After that, choices become clear. Decisions get made, and lives change for the better. I had to admit that maybe some words on that list might shed a little light for me, too.

Eventually, I narrowed down my own core values to three: **Autonomy**, **Harmony**, and **Kindness**.

Well, that's nice. But what does that even mean?

It means that whether I'm screwing up everything or cruising along merrily, those paradigms create my natural, gravitational pull. They guide my instincts. I associate them in different ways with different aspects of my life, but they always call out to me—seductive by some intangible measure in my head.

Most of us can hear the call of our values to some degree. At the very least, we usually have some awareness when we're betraying them. The challenge comes when we have to decide how (and whether) to respond to that tension.

In my experience, there are two common and highly efficient ways to betray your values. (Though I'm sure, if you're inventive, you could come up with more.)

The first is to heed them via destructive means. *Sabotage.* I shine at this one, as you will see.

The second is to deny them. *See no evil, hear no evil.* Ignorance is bliss . . . until they catch up with you and take you down like a linebacker in your blind spot. A client of mine will generously provide us with a window into this one.

I offer these two examples in a spirit of transparency. Like everyone else, my clients and I are adept at undermining ourselves via both methods. Champions, in fact. We're very proud.

EXAMPLE #1

SABOTAGE: VALUES GONE ROGUE

A million years ago, in what seems like another lifetime, I had a nasty and persistent eating disorder. I've written about it before, but what follows isn't about eating disorders. It's about how I moved past it and what that experience taught me about control, patience, and healing. It's about What Mattered to me while in the midst of that dissonance and how the magnetic pull of What Mattered extricated me from what seemed like an impossible situation.

But what does any of this have to do with **Autonomy**, **Harmony**, and **Kindness**? Sounds like some hippy nonsense, right?

Well, here's the thing. I was wrecked by this disorder in my late teens and much of my twenties. There were several medical and psychological issues at play that cannot be minimized. I was clinically depressed. At twenty-one, I'd been dumped nearly at the altar, three weeks before moving to New York City. I was busking, temping, and cocktail waitressing for cash. There was a lot going on that I am not medically qualified to address.

What I do know, from the safe distance I currently occupy, is that I felt catastrophically out of control. But I was also *free* for the first time in my life. I was free of parents, school, and childhood, and there was nothing in the world I wanted more than that. **Autonomy**—the freedom to make my own blissful and sometimes-destructive choices. I could free fall through New York City nightclubs and filthy alleys with all kinds of unhealthy habits and a heart cracked open, but as long as I was free to do it my way, I was more myself than I'd ever been.

Every step I took was painfully out of balance, because the vehicle for my existence—my body—was anathema to me. Food was the devil's spawn, and, at the same time, it was the easiest source of relief I could find. When I gave myself over to food, I was in **Harmony**. A giant burrito and a dozen doughnuts could put me into a coma that would last the night. For those few hours, I didn't have to rage. I could melt. I could doze and deal with the ramifications later.

Messed up? Yes. Fulfilling my needs? Also yes. There, I found a peaceful place with a sugar high and a full belly. The outside world left me alone, but the loathing that resulted, as I opened my eyes the following morning, was perverse.

One of my values was missing. One crucial thing was not happening in this delicate exchange. I was not being **Kind**—to myself, anyway. I was intentionally kind to strangers who shoved me out of the way on the subway and to patrons who grabbed my ass at the cocktail bar where I worked. To them, I gave the benefit of the doubt that something inside of them was too wounded to know better (I managed to do that only some of the time; let's be real), but, when it came to me, I was ruthless and unforgiving—all-out cruel.

My nature is peace and equanimity. Call me a chump if you want, but my predisposition is to be as **Kind** as I can, as often as I can, to as many living creatures as I can. But, at that juncture, I was the exception to my own rule.

Kindness brought me back. **Harmony** and **Autonomy** had found cozy places in the twisted nooks and crannies of my behavior—in both productive and unproductive ways—but **Kindness** was pulling on my sleeve like a neglected toddler pleading for attention. **Kindness** nudged at the outer reaches of my awareness, telling me that I would have to appreciate my body and mind just as they were before I could change them in any meaningful way.

Kindness reminded me that my heart was broken, and I didn't know who I was or what I wanted to do, and it was going to take a minute to figure it out. And if food gave me a little bit of comfort, that choice needed to be okay for the time being—or I'd be caught in a cycle of food addiction forever. And, as I began to listen, **Kindness** revealed that fresh air, sunlight, time with friends, and moving my body were all legit medicine.

Heeding that gravitational pull, healthier manifestations of **Harmony** and **Autonomy** found their footing, as well. It took a while, longer than it had to. The path was patchy and uneven. I twisted ankles and fell flat on my face numerous times, but the further I went, the more familiar and manageable it became. I was following whiffs of What Mattered, and that instinct got me where I needed to go. But if I had more clearly understood what was driving me at the time, what I was actually hungry for, I could have eased the way. I could have administered a steady dose of reinforcements specifically designed to meet those needs, healthy habits in the form of simple pleasures—and I could have arrived a lot sooner.

The values that lure me—those three sirens—are also at the heart of my career choices. I became a personal trainer to learn how to be in **Harmony** with my body, rather than trying to overpower it, and to help others do the same. But I was uncomfortable with the idea of working for a gym. I wanted to work in a place that celebrated people of all shapes and sizes, but I couldn't find that perspective anywhere in gym culture in the mid-2000s. My notion of the wildly divergent forms fitness can take didn't conform to that mold. Instead, I pieced together a small, beloved, ragtag clientele and worked out of my one-bedroom apartment in East Los Angeles before moving into a larger space in Nashville, Tennessee.

Autonomy was a top priority from the beginning—so I could determine my own schedule and, more importantly, impart messages uniquely suited to each of my clients about wellness as a form of healing and a source of life.

And **Kindness**—the whole, roundabout pursuit always comes back to **Kindness**—for myself, my clients, and a culture that struggles to see beauty and wisdom in the diversity of our unique bodies and minds.

The work I do scratches the itch I have for all three of those values.

We go after what we need to feel safe and secure, stimulated, alive, and at peace. That's just being human. Sometimes we use methods that aren't so healthy—and then those methods become habits. But if we tune in to what's missing, to what we're aching for, we can find ways to fill those gaps in healthier, more productive ways.

EXAMPLE #2
SEE NO EVIL, HEAR NO EVIL: STONE-COLD DENIAL

A client of mine offers a different example of what can happen when we depart from What Matters.

Let's call her Nina: she is thirty-eight years old, single, ambitious, an animal lover, and a concert aficionado. [20] And let's say it's 5:41 p.m. on a Tuesday night. Nina enters my office, eleven minutes late by her count. She drops her purse on the table, fumbles with her keys, spills her water, drops her cell phone, and slumps on the couch. She just finished a ten-hour workday, and yesterday she worked fifteen hours. Nina's job demands early mornings that flow into late nights. She is a mid-level manager with a team of fourteen people reporting to her. She loves her job, but she is also one sleepless night away from throwing her computer through her window.

Nina tells me she is eight months overdue for dentist and eye doctor appointments. She doesn't know the last time she took her car in for an oil change. She's been skipping workouts and shortchanging her dog on walks. Her romantic life is nonexistent. She is exhausted, distracted, frustrated, and constantly putting out fires. She picks up the slack for everyone else at work; their obligations somehow qualify as more important than hers. And today she realized that, for the first time in her life, she missed a rent payment. By two weeks.

What is driving her? What is her gravitational pull? Why does she sacrifice her own basic needs to accommodate the needs of others? How much of her situation is under her control? How much is not, and what can she do to change it?

Nina values **Preparedness, Expertise**, and **Connection**. Honoring these values is the key to making a different choice. If Nina values **Preparedness**, but overcompensating in one area of her life (work) has destroyed her ability to function in another (taking decent care of herself), she is betraying this core value. Being **Prepared** for everyone else has destroyed her ability to be anywhere near **Prepared** for herself. She has abandoned her own well-being in the service of others, and now everyone is suffering.

At work, she is snapping at subordinates and setting an example that burnout is the status quo. At home, her dog is barking at the walls. Her landlord is short on cash. Her car is running on sludge . . . or whatever weirdness happens when the oil doesn't get changed. Meanwhile, her teeth are rotting, and she just might run into you in traffic because she can't see the street signs anymore. And, of course, emails are piling up at work, as much, if not more, than ever before.

Her tabletop is wobbly. She needs her sugar packets to balance things out, but they're lost and crumpled at the bottom of her purse.

Nina knows what's important. She knows why she feels distracted and misaligned. She knows she is directing her values into one part of her life at the expense of the rest, and that this approach is unsustainable. Her instincts are to be ready, knowledgeable, and united with the people she loves and respects. She can honor those instincts by finding ways to apply them not only to her work life, but to her private life, as well. She can become an **Expert** at taking better care of herself by researching opportunities to insert small changes into her routine. She can **Prepare** herself with the necessary logistics to achieve those little victories throughout her days and allot her time so she can better **Connect** with everyone and everything she cares about.

Elevating those values will ease her stress and focus her mind. She'll be able to do her job, to work and live, and set a better example for her staff—and her dog too. The principles that matter to her can help her shift that balance, to show up reliably—**Prepared, Expert**, and ready to **Connect**.

An Interested Listener

When we betray our values, we feel like yesterday's garbage. When we honor them—even if the circumstances around us are collapsing—we are, at the very least, grounded in truth.

But once we know what those values are, how do we go about honoring them?

We listen. And respond.

In *Bread for the Journey*, Henri J. M. Nouwen wrote, "To listen is very hard, because it asks of us so much interior stability that we no longer need to prove ourselves by speeches, arguments, statements, or declarations. True listeners . . . are free to receive, to welcome, to accept."[21]

You know your coping mechanisms well. You rely on them. Whether beneficial or destructive, the ones you return to are, most likely, easy to implement and well within your grasp. You have a system. You may not like it, but you do have a system in place to meet your needs.

To create a different system, you need some basic information, and the way to get it is to stop making speeches and arguments; stop assuming; stop talking down to yourself; stop pontificating about all the ways you should or should not be, or the things you should or should not be doing—and listen to the messages your body is sending.

Listen. Receive. And respond—with an alternative that fills those same needs.

You may not know, yet, exactly what you value or what you're hungry for, but you do know when something feels off. You know when it's time for a fourteen-day course of Prilosec because your stomach won't stop burning—and those alarm bells signal all kinds of useful information. These signals feel terrible. Frequently, they hurt, either physically or emotionally, but they provide you with valuable insight into what sets you off and how your body responds. They offer the seeds of truth you need to start making changes—if you're willing to play the part of an interested listener.

Baseline

You have arrived at your baseline, at the bottom of a beautiful valley, dotted with wildflowers. (And no, you don't have allergies, Grumpus.)

Revisit the list of Reasons for Doing All the Things (page 42). Take a look at the words you selected and see if they fit into general categories. Are there similarities? Do they echo each other or overlap? Are you simultaneously **Trustworthy** and **Honest**? Are you both **Responsible** and **Disciplined**? See if you can organize your words into three columns.

Category #1	Category #2	Category #3
achievement	ambition	success
adventure	excitement	vibration
balance	clarity	determination
challenge	connection	excitement
community	family	fitness
honesty	honor	love
legacy	growth	gratitude

And then, narrow them down to one header for each category, one word that rings most true for you, right now. You can always go back and change them later.

THIS MATTERS:

- *ambitious*
- *compassionate*
- *reliable*

These are your initial core values. They might be spot on and guide you forevermore, or they might change over time or turn out to be masquerading as something else. You might find that you are fulfilling them in healthy or unhealthy ways. Either way, they are a perfect place to start.

These three principles are the basis of your gravitational pull.

If they feel good for now, carry them around for a while. Tuck them into a safe place in your backpack. You never know when you'll need a little boost to keep things on the level.

What are some ways you're living your values right now, either productively or destructively?

....

....

....

....

What are some ways you're denying them?

....

....

....

....

Chapter 4

Easy Like

Melted Butter

The valley before you is carved by a long, flowing river, winding as far as you can see. The water appears smooth and navigable. At the river's edge, you find a dock with an array of boats anchored and waiting. Each one has a sign that says, "Choose me!"

There is a sailboat bobbing silently in the breeze, a motorboat with its engine humming, and a pontoon boat with a protective awning covering the stern. Beyond the smaller boats, there is a fishing vessel, a submarine, a cabin cruiser with all the basic creature comforts, and a large yacht with deck chairs and champagne flutes at the ready.

You wander from boat to boat, exploring the possibilities at hand. Do you climb aboard one, or head back up the hill toward your intersection and the familiar quiet of your house? The hill heading back to home base is long and steep. *Too steep*, you decide. So far, forward motion has served you well. You are balanced and focused, and the water is calm. You choose a boat and step on board. Pushing off from the dock, you watch the hill and valley disappear as you float (or speed) away from the bank.

As you settle in, you find a picnic basket with fruit and wine, sparkling water and chocolates, nuts and cheeses. At the bottom of the basket is a loaf of fresh bread, a butter knife, and a small, glass dish of hand-churned butter. (Veganize or de-gluten this situation if you wish. Add some beer. Whatever you like. It's your boat and your basket.)

With great satisfaction, you rip off a hunk of steaming, hot, homemade bread, and spread a pat of the warm butter over it. In this chapter, you get to explore what comes easily to you—easy like melted butter.

This part of the journey is all about your strengths—the skills you call on without a second thought; the ways you approach the world that make life doable. These strengths are your basic tools. They are the hammer, drill, and level you'll use to build the platform in your orb and to reinforce your home. They are the gadgets and gizmos you'll need to build safety rails and a protective net to catch you when you fall, bounce, and regain your balance.

Treasure

Re-energized now with food and drink, relaxed and rested, you peer over the edge of your boat. The water has grown murky with silt and sand, but somewhere beneath the surface, you see an irresistible sparkle of something familiar. You hesitate. Is this worth exploring? You'd rather not get wet, and what if you're just imagining things? *Oh, fuck it. This trip has been bizarre enough already. Why not?!* On an impulse, you dive in and swim straight for the riverbed, where you find a cache of riches.

Triumphantly, you rise to the surface with a burst of enthusiasm, your arms full of treasure. You climb back into the boat—soaked, out of breath, replete with objects long-lost, and more alive than you have felt in ages. These are your childhood passions, a collection of everything you loved and excelled at as a kid. When looking for the things you do best, you'll find clues in whatever came naturally when you were small. For many, childhood was far from ideal, but even if yours was less than perfect, where did you thrive? What did you cherish? What got you excited or gave you peace? These passions don't need to impress anyone else. They don't require trophies or accolades. All that matters is that they meant a great deal to you as a child.

If you loved basketball, why? Was it the stats, the teamwork, feeling strong and fast, or something else about it that lit your fire? If you loved ballet, was it the music? The precise movements? The chance to practice with friends, or the glow of performing for an audience? If you babysat younger siblings or neighborhood kids, did you enjoy a sense of leadership, an opportunity to create activities, or just plain cash-money in your first-ever bank account?

Whatever your passions were—drawing, animals, reading and writing, chess, singing, soccer, science, cooking, magic—put them on paper and explore the characteristics that came to you so distinctly. Pull them out of that mucky water, shine them up, and display them proudly on the bow of your ship.

Passion #1:

....

Why did you love it?

....

....

Passion #2:

....

Why did you love it?

....

....

....

Passion #3:

....

Why did you love it?

....

....

....

Now we're talking. You've got yourself a basket of snacks, a beautiful day, and a full-on display of everything you ever loved as a kid. *Ah, memories.*

The boat floats around a sharp bend into a narrow tributary. The banks are overgrown with trees and brush, beautiful but wild, and through this short passage, you find yourself musing on early adulthood.

When you think back on yourself at eighteen or twenty-two years old, what were you good at? If this person were a niece or nephew looking for guidance, what would you tell them about their best qualities? What characteristics are you proud of in them?

....

....

....

....

....

The People You Love

Here, the tributary opens up into a vast lake with crystal clear water, and, suddenly, you can see for miles. You're feeling rooted and very much yourself—a deeper, more vibrant, and complex version of the young adult you once were. Your clothes and hair have begun to dry, untamed. There's no pretense here, no one to impress. You realize this is exactly how you feel when you are with your person—the person who lets you be yourself and loves you through every achievement and every stumble. This person may be your best friend, partner, spouse, sister or brother, parent, or whoever else puts helium in your balloon and lets you fly.

It sure would be nice if they were here right now, you think. They could help you grow that salvaged trove of childhood interests into a fully developed, all-grown-up appreciation for what you have to offer. They could help you identify the natural strengths that help you get the job done: skills that smooth out your life from the center like a pat of melted butter.

You know what your person is good at. You can see their best qualities, no problem, but seeing your own is considerably harder. So, to make things easy, let's flip the mirror for a minute and focus on them.

Think about the person you selected: What do you admire in them? What approaches do they take to situations they face? Are they passionate? Caring? Imaginative or insightful? Resilient? Confident? Determined? What do you value about their friendship? What comes easily to them, and in exactly which ways are they crushing it?

Check out this list of qualities to see which ones best describe your person. And, as always, insert your own words as you wish.

Crushing It Skill Set

Adaptable	Dedicated	Innovative	Playful
Ambitious	Determined	Insightful	Positive
Artistic	Devoted	Intelligent	Proactive
Athletic	Empathetic	Intuitive	Realistic
Calm	Energetic	Kind	Reliable
Candid	Flexible	Leader	Resilient
Caring	Focused	Meticulous	Resourceful
Charismatic	Funny	Motivated	Respectful
Clear-headed	Generous	Organized	Responsible
Competitive	Good Listener	Open-minded	Sincere
Confident	Hard-working	Outspoken	Smart
Considerate	Helpful	Passionate	Social Butterfly
Courageous	Honest	Patient	Problem Solver
Creative	Humble	Perceptive	Team Player
Curious	Imaginative	Persistent	Thoughtful
Decisive	Independent	Persuasive	Tough

....

Name your person:

....

Name their strengths:

1. ....

2. ....

3. ....

Now do it again. Pick somebody else who puts you at ease. What do you see in them that makes them one of your favorite people?

Name your person:

....

Name their strengths:

1. ....

2. ....

3. ....

Do this with as many people as you like. The qualities you have listed are ones you revere in your most beloved people. Their strengths may overlap with your own, or they may complement you by filling in gaps where you aren't so strong. Either way, they are worth noting. It's easy for us to see strengths in others, but they can be notoriously difficult to see in ourselves.

So, let's flip that mirror back around.

Your Turn

Your phone has been safely tucked away in your backpack this whole trip. Until now, that electronic window to the outside world seemed like a distraction, but you can't figure this one out alone. It's hard enough to know what "strengths" actually are—much less which ones you possess. It's time to enlist the help of your friends and family.

With a simple text message, you can gather intel about how others see you and the contributions you make in the lives of the people who love you. Dig out the phone, and text three people from different areas of your life a straightforward question: "What would you say are my three greatest strengths?" Their answers may surprise you. Fill them in below.

(If this feels uncomfortable, you can try to guess what your people might say, but that's not nearly as fun. Before you back out, consider starting the conversation with the strengths you see in them. Everybody loves a compliment, especially when it's true.)

PERSON #1

1.

2.

3.

PERSON #2

1.

2.

3.

PERSON #3

1.

2.

3.

Now we're getting somewhere. You've got a feel for how you are perceived by the people who know you best—and what they value in you.

You tuck your phone away again and settle back into the view of the lake and your childhood accomplishments. Here you are with your unruly hair and your fancy boat. You've got your values in your bag, and you just remembered you're pretty damn good at some things.

So answer me this, if you don't mind.

What do you like about yourself?

WHOA. Too hard. Too personal. Not comfortable with that question!

Come on now, get to bragging. There's no one here, after all. It's just you and your boat.

I'm sure you're pretty accomplished at beating yourself up for tiny missteps; good at second-guessing yourself, too; maybe also good at trashing yourself for eating the wrong thing, working too much, or not dressing right. I'm sure you excel at those and many other unhelpful intellectual mind games—but that's not the point here. We're talking about what comes naturally—easy like melted butter.

So, I'll ask again: what do you like about yourself?

What are you unquestionably good at? What do you see from this perch on your boat—and through the eyes of your friends and family—that you couldn't see before? Take a look at that Crushing It list one more time (page 61). What is your modus operandi? Which strengths belong to you?

I'VE GOT THIS.

- ....
- ....
- ....

On Course

With your values guiding you and your strengths on full display, you find yourself getting antsy. You can't stay here on this boat forever. I mean, you can, but do you want to? It's a bit lonely. And constricting. You've got fresh confidence and an increasing urge to use your skills to go after what you want.

You have ideas about your house! The orb, too. Maybe even a little landscaping. This is exciting. You're all hopped up on good vibrations, and you don't want to wait another minute to get moving. But, you're stuck out here in the middle of nowhere on this boat!

Gah! Unfurl that sail, push the throttle all the way down, or put pedal to the metal to get back to shore. You've got pressing matters to tend to. Set your course. You know exactly where you're going.

Arriving at your destination, you dock the boat and leave it behind for another passenger on another day. You know this harbor well. It's the Town of Favorite Things—a place full of everything you love.

Chapter 5

For the Love of It

J ust beyond the boardwalk, you are greeted by a sign, that reads:

Love is like infinity . . .

Infinity just is, and that's the way I think love is, too.

—Mr. Rogers

Aww, Mr. Rogers! Who doesn't love Mr. Rogers?

In fact, all the things you ever loved are right here in this lakeside village. Your obsession with public art and fascination with strangers sitting on park benches are woven into the fabric of this place. The streets are saturated with your affection for space exploration, hot showers, unexplained coincidences, and indigo nail polish.

Standing at the edge of town, you limber up. You got cramped on that boat, and it's time to go exploring.

What you're good at is important, for sure, but *what you love* is the greatest motivator you have. When you love something, you go after it without hesitation. You crave it. There is no separating you from your passion for your Favorite Things, whatever they may be: dancing, baking, beekeeping, or studying the textile trade routes of the ancient world.

The Town of Favorite Things is a hamlet of your authentic interests, fluctuating from endearment to fascination. It's a collection of activities, people, places, and things that bring you joy, comfort, or satisfaction. The more you engage with them, the healthier and more balanced you are. Some may not be readily available in your regular life—due to time or monetary constraints—but here you have free reign to indulge and, in time, to find smaller, more accessible versions of them.

Honey's Gospel of Positive Reinforcement

T he mayor of the Town of Favorite Things is an aging Labrador retriever named Honey. She is a wise, old soul with a litter of local pups always nipping at her heels. She understands the puppies and their needs. She recognizes that sometimes they *believe* they love things that aren't good for them—like eating mulch, chasing wasps, and biting each other's ears until they bleed—but the pups learn over time that their Favorite Things, the ones they truly love, are soft, warm beds, other creatures to snuggle with, reliable routines in their days, exercise for their bodies, challenges for their brains, satisfied bellies, and treats when they do something helpful.

So she feeds them those Things, and the puppies grow into strong, healthy dogs. Eventually, they are adopted by people passing through town and taken into the wider world to preach her Gospel of Positive Reinforcement.

"Our bodies are sources of pleasure," she tells the little ones. "We cannot conquer them. We can only feed them—with love, structure, and little bits of kindness. There may be some things you 'like' that also make you feel sick or frustrated. Do not be misled. These are not your Favorite Things. Your Favorite Things bring you peace, connection, or excitement. They combine wellness and pleasure. They give you life."

Oh, and when the Humans come to town! Ha! The Humans. She gets a kick out of that. She cocks her head and watches them wandering the streets. Most of the time, they don't even know where they are. They're too busy *doing things*, all worked up about something they call "adulting"—doing taxes, fighting the school board, repairing the HVAC, plucking their eyebrows, paying the bills, and finishing reports. All of those—and many more serious, grown-up troubles—are important to the Humans. They worry a lot. To manage the stress, they rely on some habits that bring them short-term pleasure and long-term pain. And their bodies pay the price, especially when they lose track of their Favorite Things.

Many of their responsibilities are beyond their control, she thinks. *But it's such a shame. They have control over so much more than they realize.* By "control," she means *access* to more resources for healing than they recognize—and that access comes through the love they already possess for things that bring them to life.

Some of their satisfaction comes through comfort and some by conquest. Humans are exceedingly good at accomplishing enormous, challenging tasks, but they have a hard time remembering that the activities, people, and objects that fill them with wonder are tonics that make them well. They struggle to see that life is smoother when they roll with their innate momentum, and the simpler the pleasure, the better.

Walking, breathing, stretching, touching, seeing, speaking, listening, eating, and sleeping are the most powerful therapies at their disposal. Every one of these creature comforts makes Humans (and puppies, too) more creative, productive, focused, and happy. But the people are all wrapped up in "adulting," so they forget.

Lucky for them, the sun switches on every morning, and so do their bodies, with infinite (and free) resources for feeling well. Every now and then, a Human wakes up in the Town of Favorite Things and realizes what they've been missing all along.

Honey has a hard time understanding why Humans believe they have to suffer to get bodies that make them happy. *Come to think of it*, she wonders, *why do they have to "get" new bodies at all? They have them already, and their bodies bring such pleasure!* They taste chocolate fudge. They hug. They stretch in the morning. They sleep. They soak up the sun and make art and join hands and climb mountains and build buildings and make love (again and again) in waves of velvety ecstasy. (She saw it happen once when the Humans forgot she was in the room.)

Humans can enjoy all those things—if they allow themselves. But most of the time, they don't. They're too busy bossing their bodies around, talking down to them, telling them how to look and behave, and reprimanding themselves for being ugly and unacceptable. To remedy the flaws they perceive, they fixate on deprivation, on what they *can't* do instead of what they can.

Honey waits for her chance to offer what comfort she can. She wishes the Humans would let "wellness" be about actual wellness: pleasure, peace, connection, contribution, play, balance, and reducing their pain. She knows those comforts are what they're after anyway, even when they try to get them by austere and rigid means. The Humans are just trying to take better care of themselves, so she guides them gently, redirecting them to build new habits on the bedrock of their Favorite Things. It's much easier that way.

There are only three laws she enforces here:
1. **Every new habit, every reinforcement, must be chosen for the love of it.**
2. **Every new habit must be broken down into bite-sized bits.**
3. **Every bit of progress must be rewarded.**

She requires strict compliance with these rules while visiting and strongly recommends—with her chin on your lap and big brown eyes looking up at you—that you abide by them wherever you roam.

Judge and Jury

Your body is the conduit for every satisfying experience you will ever have. It is the judge and jury that decides if you truly love something. Your neck and shoulders know if you enjoy how you spend your time. When you think of spin class, modern art, or throwing dinner parties, your gut knows if you love it or hate it.

People thrive when they do things they care about in ways they love, even if those things aren't necessarily easy. They pick a problem and make a change for the better *because it feels good*—because they need and want to—not because they're "supposed to."

Sometimes the things we need to do are hard, scary, or monotonous. But, if they are connected to What Matters and supported by skills we're good at, they aren't so awful after all—especially if those challenges are surrounded by ever-increasing doses of simple pleasures.

Taking care of an aging parent or a newborn baby can be exhausting, but we do it anyway because it matters. We love our people, and they need our help. We reap the benefits of those relationships but only if we don't resent the person in our care. The easiest way to avoid feeling resentment is to make sure there is adequate time to read or sleep or go out with friends, but caregivers are often not afforded these luxuries. Our networks make this time for renewal possible.

Going back to school for an advanced degree can be overwhelming. If we're excited about our field, the effort is not only worth it, it's exhilarating. But to learn, there must be time for our minds to wander and assimilate the information. We need brain space: time for hiking, a movie, or a nap. Otherwise, the excitement shrivels and dies, and learning becomes a marathon of one task after another.

Starting a business can be intimidating. After my client, Linnet, was pushed out of a high-pressure job, she decided to pursue a lifelong dream of starting her own one-woman floral farming and design business, Green Linnet.[22] She spends her days planting seeds and pulling weeds, and she loves it. But she will also injure her shoulder and stress out over billing if she forgets to plant the functional reinforcements that make her work possible—like rotator cuff exercises and marketing plans. Those support systems aren't so tedious after all, because her Favorite Thing is gardening. She gets to do it all day long—and pay her bills—and finishes in time to pick up her kids from school. The reinforcements become part of the routine, pipelines for pleasure.

So here you are in town, gathering information to reinforce the infrastructure that supports your body and mind. As you begin to rebuild the walls and the floor—as you remodel the layout of your home to better suit your needs and pad your orb to make the freefalls more comfortable—the updated designs must be fashioned to quench your thirsts and soothe your appetites. Otherwise, the whole thing is a bust: you've broken the law and best get on out of the Town of Favorite Things. *Go directly to jail. Do not pass GO. Do not collect $200.*[23]

There is love in your life somewhere. There is probably some hate, too, and there is definitely at least a little indifference. Your body knows how to distinguish between them. It is the guide that will show you the way.

Your Favorite Things

L ook around. What streets and businesses are in this town? Is there a library? A grocery store in walking distance? A craft store? A trail to climb? Nightlife? Local restaurants? A school your kids can love? A coffee shop? A bike path? A bookstore? A dog park? A town square to practice your stump speech? A cake-decorating class? A weekly meeting place for your brain-trust of magnificent human beings? What is the architecture of the buildings like? What kind of transportation do you have?

Honey has some questions for you. As you ponder them, check in with your body, and you will know if your answers are truthful.

What is one thing you wish you could do every day for the rest of your life?

....

What other activities can you not get enough of? What makes you lose track of time?

....

....

....

What rituals open your lungs and soften your neck?

....

....

....

What are you looking forward to in the next six months?

....

....

....

What are three small things you already do regularly to reinforce your well-being, just because you enjoy them? These can be anything from tap dancing to flossing to calling your best friend on Sundays.

1. ....

2. ....

3. ....

Emoji Volcano

Um, wait a minute. Hold on. I know you're focused on the lovey-dovey happy stuff right now, but you may want to turn around and take a look behind you. Your lake, full of crystal clear water and insights from the past, is over there. But to your left . . . yeah . . . that's a monstrous, steaming volcano towering over you, with red slits for eyes and emoji devil horns protruding ominously from each side of the lava-filled gash.

This volcano is a roiling brew of negative rumination, midnights on social media, too many hours at the office, quick-fix diets, destructive vices, fast-fashion clothing that shrinks the first time you wash it, calorie-counting apps, and overall burnout. It's a boiling vat of all the ways we neglect, abuse, and underestimate our bodies.

If I may say so, that volcano appears to be threatening your town with all of your Favorite Things in it. With one more spark—one more absurd concession that you and your body are not good enough—it could blow, covering your happy place with molten lava and destroying everything in its path.

You gotta go.

But don't forget what Mr. Rogers said. The things we love are infinite. They travel with us no matter where we go. If you know what yours are, you can find them anywhere.

Take a final look around. You can't stay here, but you can take your Favorite Things with you.

In the following chart, make a list of the activities and pastimes you love—and where you can find them in both micro- and macro-form. If you love to cook, maybe the micro-version involves going to a farmers' market or trying a new recipe with a friend once a week. Maybe the macro-version involves jetting off to Italy for a month-long cooking course.

There is infinite room for these items, so you can keep coming back to this page (or make your own elsewhere) when more things you love occur to you. It's an ever-growing inventory. This is the nourishment you will need, in doses large and small, to keep you going. It is the raw material that will reinforce your every move.

FAVORITE THING

Micro-version

Macro-version

FAVORITE THING

Micro-version

Macro-version

FAVORITE THING

Micro-version

Macro-version

FAVORITE THING

Micro-version

Macro-version

FAVORITE THING

Micro-version

Macro-version

Chapter 6

Future TBD

Night is falling. You're perched atop a cliff at a safe distance from the volcano, where you can survey the landscape you have traveled. Lights are on in the Town of Favorite Things. The harbor is glowing with string lights along the docks. The volcano, reflected in the dark shimmer of the lake, is quiet for now. Beyond the water, you can see the hill and valley you came from and your ten-way intersection at the top—barely visible—with your house just beyond, looking like a grain of sand.

The journey, so far, has provided you with crucial information and supplies.

You know what matters to you and can use that knowledge to direct your course.

You know what you're good at.

You have identified the things you love, how they nourish you, and where they can be found in small and large doses to fuel your next steps.

To What End?

But what's the purpose of all of this journeying, in the end? Happiness?

Daniel Gilbert, Edgar Pierce Professor of Psychology at Harvard University and author of *Stumbling on Happiness*, has done decades of research into what makes us happy and how good (or bad) we are at predicting those factors.[24] He proposes that future happiness is an amorphous concept that is notoriously difficult to nail down. His research suggests that the human imagination is largely inept at predicting two things:

1. How events will unfold when/if they come to pass, and
2. How we will feel about them when they do happen.

According to Dr. Gilbert, one way to remedy this is to seek the experience of people who have already accomplished whatever we imagine we would like to do. Gauging their happiness levels is a surprisingly reliable way to predict our own future satisfaction. If you want to be an advertising executive or a doggy day care owner, ask someone who is already doing it what it's like. Even better, as the observations of these mentors ping off your nervous system, check in with your body, the judge and jury, to see if their perspectives and values resonate with your own.

Most of us resist this path, believing instead that we can determine better for ourselves what will make us happy, based on assumptions we hold about who we will be in the distant future. The problem is that we are not clairvoyant. We are terrible at predicting how our perspectives will shift over time—how we'll feel if we detour down alternate paths or if events beyond our control change our trajectory. But this shortcoming of human imagination is not all bad. It means that later we'll be different than we are now. We *do* change. In fact, we change a lot more than we think we will.

In her memoir, *Becoming*, Michelle Obama writes about the consuming drive she had in her younger life to become a lawyer. Born on the South Side of Chicago to parents who did not have the opportunity to go to college, she graduated from Princeton University and Harvard Law School, gaining confidence and proving her competency to herself (and everyone else) along the way. But just a few years after law school, rising through the ranks at a powerful corporate law firm back in Chicago, she discovered that the future she had dreamed of, the one she pursued so ferociously, didn't turn out to be the life she wanted at all. It didn't match the person she had become.

"I hated being a lawyer," she writes. "I wasn't suited to the work. I felt empty doing it, even if I was plenty good at it. This was a distressing thing to admit, given how hard I'd worked and how in debt I was. In my blinding drive to excel, in my need to do things perfectly, I'd missed the signs and taken the wrong road . . . Somehow, in all my years of schooling, I hadn't managed to think through my own passions and how they might match up with work I found meaningful . . . I couldn't continue to live with my own complacency."[25]

This is like running head-on into a glass door. *Thwack!* I don't know about you, but I've hit plenty of unforeseen glass doors like this in my life. *Crap. This doesn't feel like I thought it would.*

On an episode of the NPR podcast *Hidden Brain* with Shankar Vedantam, Dr. Gilbert describes how this tendency to underestimate how much we will change shows up in the research. "Look," he says, "we all know eighteen-year-olds are crazy. They think they are who they are, that they're going to be that way forever. They have crazy hairstyles and tattoos that they believe they're going to want for the rest of their lives, and old people like me snicker and say, 'You're going to see,' because eighteen-year-olds underestimate how different they're going to be when they're twenty-eight. We showed this in our experiment by asking eighteen-year-olds to tell us how much they would change in the next ten years and asking twenty-eight-year-olds to tell us how much they had changed in the last ten years. In a perfectly rational world, those numbers would be the same—and they weren't. Eighteen-year-olds thought they would change very little. Twenty-eight-year-olds reported having changed a lot. But what's so interesting about the study is that it's also true with fifty-eight-year-olds and sixty-eight-year-olds. Fifty-eight-year-olds think, 'Okay I'm done. I'm cooked. It'll just be me, maybe a little flabbier, more wrinkles, but I'm the guy I'm gonna be.' Sixty-eight-year-olds look back at the last ten years and think, 'Wow, have I changed!'"[26]

So we're all running smack into our own glass doors. At least we're doing it together, though. We're not isolated in these delusions.

The idea that our brains are fundamentally deficient at predicting who we will be or what we will want in the future is disconcerting. If we're projecting fantasy worlds that may or may not align with reality, how can we even begin to decide what's next? Are we striving for the right things?

Disconcerting? Sure. But disabling? Not so much. The opposite, in fact.

Let's take this concept to the extreme. Let's say you have absolutely no idea what will make you happy in old age, no clue. You're blindly feeling your way toward an oblique, nebulous future, and nothing you believe today will hold true when you are older. Your existence is one big maze with a beginning and an end—with no concept of how to get from here to there. What measure of control does that leave you with? How can you strategize? How are you supposed to know what to do *now* to make life good *later*?? *I'm a planner, dammit! I need to know!*

You may not be able to predict the future with accuracy, but you can cozy up to the present and double down on what you know to be true, here and now. What if the goal isn't happiness, anyway? What if the goal is groundedness? Authenticity? Or presence? Pick whatever word you like for it, but the bottom line is truth: your honest self, no better or worse, just you—at peace and without pretense.

A lifetime of meaningful choices plus a steady drip of small pleasures equals a future that feels like home. As Grand Pabbie, the Troll King, says in *Frozen II*, "When one can't see the future, all one can do is the next right thing."[27]

The power to shape the future lives in the choices directly in front of us. If the decisions you make along the way are from the heart—rooted in awareness of who you are and what you want to offer—every choice will be clearer and each outcome will lead to the next.

Your body knows the answer, remember? Even in the toughest circumstances, when all hell has broken loose, you know in the pit of your stomach which way feels best. It may not be effortless. The path may require a lot of work, time, or effort, but it will also be honest. Living this way, you can't help but end up somewhere that feels right.

Who knows how long you'll live or what the future holds? You don't have much control over accidents or cancer. You can't be sure you'll make it to old age, but you might. In fact, you likely will. According to the World Health Organization, the average life expectancy in North America, Europe, and most industrialized countries is about seventy-seven years. Global average life expectancy is around seventy-two years.[28] Calculating backward (and giving yourself a few extra years for good behavior), how long does that give you?

Let's say you have twenty, thirty, or fifty years to go. That gives you two, three, or five lifetimes yet to live. Your current perspective is not the same as it was before—let's hope not, anyway—and it's not the same as it will be later, either.

By making it this far, you have self-identified as a seeker. You're curious about your options and willing to explore. You're motivated and eager to deviate from what's not working. You've come to this cliff with a birds-eye view of where you came from. This arrival, in and of itself, is a triumph. You have achieved perspective.

Liquid Brick Road

You decide it's time to go home, and there are two ways to get there: You can go back the way you came, revisit challenges you've already faced, and reacquaint yourself with outcomes you know too well. Or you can press on and find a different route.

One way is well-established. The other is strange and likely unstable. The second path is unnerving but alluring. You're familiar with this feeling. It's Fear of the Unknown, a sign of evolution and the gatekeeper to everything new. If you follow this Fear, you get to find out what's on the other side, which might be beautiful and idyllic—or it might be fraught with unexpected challenges. You crack a decisive smile and take a breath. Something new and intriguing is in the works.

With that, you step away from the cliff toward the flatland before you, nudged along by momentum you can feel but cannot see. Without warning, it sweeps you through a portal and into a void.

There, you find yourself standing on a black surface that weeps color and light like gasoline on water. You take a step—and step again—gleefully watching the colors swirl away from your feet. This is the Liquid Brick Road, a solid whirlpool of purple, yellow, turquoise, and red. It's fluid, offering boundless possibilities, but it points toward a singular destination: your body house, the ultimate arbiter of what's true and what's not.

You're inclined to keep moving, but the choice to turn back is tempting. The original path is well worn; no meddlesome surprises there. You know how to negotiate it, and you know the end results.

If you want to make a change, the next section of the book will help you figure out how. If you don't, I recommend setting this mission aside for now. Make a conscious choice and put this book on a bookshelf or give it to a friend. Maybe life is too chaotic at the moment, or all this blathering on about habits and choices is annoying, or you're just a little—*SQUIRREL!!*— *what?* Oh yeah, distracted.

One way or the other, you're longing for home. Both roads will get you there, albeit in different ways with divergent outcomes. Double back if you're content with where you are. Congratulate yourself on being smart enough to make a decision that feels good, and get on with enjoying your life. There is absolutely no reason to talk yourself into attempting a change you don't even want to make in the first place. Maybe your life is pretty great as is, and the change you thought you wanted isn't that important after all. Go with that! So. Much. Easier.

But if you're going down the new path, get used to following Fear of the Unknown around like an annoying little sister. *Hey! You want to hang out with me? Where ya goin'? Whatcha doin'? Let's do something!*

You don't know what's coming next, and neither do I. But whatever it is, it's different—directed and motivated by you, by What Matters.

Throwing Paint at the Wall

So we know the following . . .
- Our predictions are flawed.
- We have no idea what will make us happy in the long run
- But we want happiness. Or truth. Or _____.

Let's play. Throw some paint at the wall and see what happiness, truth, or _____ might look like.

If you could pick an alternate future, one radically different from your current plans, what would it be?

....

....

....

....

Is there any part of that alternate life that you'd like to have a role in your current plans?

....

....

....

....

Ten years ago, what were your top priorities and what do you wish you had worried less about?

....

....

....

....

What are your top priorities now?

....

....

....

....

If your older self could look back, what might they tell you to worry less about?

....

....

....

....

Who are you when you get to be yourself? List five words for your most grounded self.

1. ....

2. ....

3. ....

4. ....

5. ....

If you're facing a significant choice—to make a change at work or in your personal life, to embark on a major project—what is your body telling you about that? How much can you achieve while staying balanced and healthy, and how much is a step too far?

....

....

....

....

There are all sorts of plausible outcomes for your older self, all kinds of ways you could turn out by the time you're four-wheeling on your Rascal scooter, but the easiest way to end up happy is to focus on "the next right thing" on your way from here to there.

Goals for ten or twenty years from now begin with a big, unwieldy vision of maybe someday: Maybe someday I'll have a job I love. Maybe someday my neck won't hurt. Maybe someday I'll have time for my art. Maybe someday I'll live somewhere better than this place. But someday comes to be through the minutiae of changes to your daily routine: One refreshed résumé. One plane ticket. One plank exercise every morning. A conversation with a mentor. A sketchbook with colored pencils. An hour spent perusing apartment rentals and job listings in a city that feels more like home.

On an episode of *On Being*, author and religious studies professor Dr. Lewis Newman told host Krista Tippett, "If you think about this in terms of a 360-degree circle, if you're headed in one direction and you turn only 1 degree or 2 degrees to the right or to the left . . . it may be a very slight turn, but over an extended period of time, if you now walk in that direction, you'll end up in an utterly different place than if you extend that line outward infinitely. And that sense of turning even slightly . . . it doesn't have to be a radical, all of a sudden transformation into a new life. It's actually a very gradual process of recognizing, 'You know, I need to pay attention . . . and move in a little different direction.'"[29]

Every big change has roots in much smaller ones. In Part II, we'll figure out which minutiae will make the biggest difference. What's Next is always related to What Matters. If you keep doing What Matters, you'll eventually figure out What's Next.

Turns out, the Liquid Brick Road was a mesmerizing shortcut, squishy and easy on the knees. You didn't have to go very far to find your best instincts. You made it. Welcome home.

PART II:

The Solution

Chapter 7

Pick Your Pleasure

G ood news—your orb is looking sturdy. The house is still standing. The exterior is holding strong, and you've gathered the supplies you'll need. Time for some structural enhancements and your own personal zoning plan.

But first, a good night's sleep.

You walk in the door, throw down your backpack, pour yourself a drink, pull the blinds, draw a bath or take a shower, and collapse under a pile of blankets. The bed feels like heaven. You rest for eight . . . ten . . . twelve hours and wake up with soft eyes before padding outside with a cup of caffeine or your favorite juice.

It's good to be home. You're reminded of the many reasons you love it here, peeling paint and all. It's comforting being back in your space, swaddled in old routines—but with that familiarity come echoes of distraction and inertia.

Your reverie lasts only as long as that first night of sleep. Now that your brain is back online, you remember all the things that have fallen through the cracks, the reasons there isn't enough time, the repairs that haven't been done, and the bevy of unhealthy habits you repeat every day at exactly the same time—familiar (and annoying) routines that seem to help maintain your equilibrium.

Your Ten Areas have blurred into a jumble of memories and aspirations. Days pass, and the snooze button derails your mornings. Your sneakers are by the door, gathering dust. The sugar cravings are back in force. Laundry and unopened emails pile up as work creeps into your evenings. At bedtime, you're hypnotized by your phone. Your budget is precarious, and you can't remember the last time you went on a date.

Why can't I change?? Why???????? You yell to the heavens, momentarily forgetting that you are not the leading character in a silent film being tied ceremoniously to a train track by a scurrilous villain with a handlebar mustache.

No, you're just you—back to being you, in your place, with your habits and your stuff. Same old story, same old situation. *Gah!* While you were out in the world, everything seemed different. You thought you would come back fixed, perfectly functional, totally at ease, a brand-new you. To your growing dismay, that doesn't seem to be the case. The perspective you gained on the road did come home with you, but it has made you more restless not less.

You have a clearer notion now of what you want, a better idea of what's possible, too, and less patience for obsolete patterns. The contrast of this new vision with your old schtick feels irritating and disjointed. You're ready for change.

Alrighty, then! Let's do this! How about you donate all your old clothes and sew yourself a whole new wardrobe by hand? Also, quit your job, find a new one, break up with your partner, get hitched to that disconcertingly attractive person who delivered your UPS packages last week, and jump right in with their family of five. You should also definitely go on a thirty-day cleanse and exercise for two hours each morning before getting the step-kids off to school and dictating your long-dormant novel to Siri on your way to work. Right. Perfect. Off you go!

No? Too much?

Okay. Maybe it's better if you come up with your own plan.

Luckily, you've done most of the work already to figure out what changes might be useful. At the very least, you have enough information to take a first crack at making some different choices. It's a journey, after all. No plan will be airtight. The best you can do, with the fresh perspective you've acquired, is take a look at the house, the orb, and your intersection—and start from there with a spirit of investigation. This is the moment to figure out what's not working and start making moves to fix it.

The Mahogany Library

L et's say you have a grand, old library in this house of yours, with walls of built-in, mahogany bookshelves and one of those rolling stepladders that lets you reach as high as needed. This house just keeps getting better.

In your library, you have volumes of information from your life, reams of kinesthetic and cerebral knowledge about each of the Ten Areas of Well-Being (page 11). Flip through some of these books to see how they feel in your hands and put them down again if they don't keep your interest. You are looking for the areas that hold the most urgency for you. The resources you find here are vast; if you try to explore them all at once, you'll get overwhelmed—and it's no fun to be overwhelmed when you just got home from a fabulous adventure.

The process isn't complicated, though. You know which areas excite you. You know which ones tempt you to read on and look deeper. Set aside any feelings of "should" or "should not." There is no such thing here.

You're looking for ingrained habits in your Ten Areas that are irksome enough to warrant attention but not so daunting that they feel hopeless. Sideline any changes that seem too difficult, and don't bother with areas that are working just fine. For example, there is no reason to answer a bunch of questions about sleep if your sleep feels great. No reason to deep dive into fitness if your workout plan is on point. And if you want to throw all the diet books on the floor and dance over their sorry remains while burning sage and drinking whiskey, have at it.

Skip around if you want. Follow your instincts and interest; they'll lead you in the right direction. Don't force your concentration. Focus wherever you like—but be wary of the seemingly obvious. Solutions (and complications) can reside in unlikely places. One area may impact another where you least expect it: it can be hard to change your diet if you're stressed at work or in a relationship. And it can be hard to sleep if you're stuffed or starving before bed.

This is your chance to take a full accounting of the terrain, to discover which roads are roughest and prepare yourself for the tumble—because none of the areas can be avoided in the end. Every road, every element of your well-being, has a role in supporting you: your body, your ambition, productivity, creativity, and peace of mind. Abundant external resources are available to help guide you, but the only solutions worth a damn—the ones that will work—come directly from you. Your process, your answers, your way.

Which areas are you curious about? Which ones are most out of sync? Explore as many as you like, and don't bother with the others. Skip them. You can always come back later to try a different path.

The rest of this chapter is a workbook with questions about each area to help you map the ground beneath your feet. Explore at whatever pace, and in whatever capacity, feels right. You might dig up some of your own insight by going back to chapter 2 to see what initial observations you made for each of the ten roads—and if this all feels too overwhelming, don't hesitate to read the rest of the book before burrowing into specific habit changes. Take all the time you like. I'll meet you in the next chapter to make a plan.

But before you bury yourself in data—*Too many questions and not enough answers!*—stand back and look at this beautiful display of books before you. Brightly colored, unbroken spines comingle with leather-bound covers and well-loved dust jackets, ripped and torn. It might take a lifetime to read all these books, but they belong to you and, together, they are dazzling. They represent a lot of accumulated wisdom. There's no rush. Just pick up one that catches your eye.

Parachute Men

As you stand there, deciding where to begin, you look up toward the ceiling and notice a toy parachute man drifting slowly from the rafters. In fact, there are three. When they land, you pick them up and discover each has a small piece of paper tied to its neck like a cape with a question printed on the back. These questions can help you figure out which area you want to look at first.

What stressors recur in your life most frequently?

....

....

....

....

If you could uproot one or two belligerent little habits, which ones would they be?

....

....

....

....

What (or who) have you been putting on the back burner even though it (or they) energizes you?

....

....

....

....

Ten Roads and Many Questions

TIME

What parts of your current routine feel great?

....

....

....

....

What times of day feel rushed, disorganized, or overwhelming?

....

....

....

....

Which specific demands during those times feel frustrating or burdensome?

....

....

....

....

What are some ways those demands could be limited or removed?

....

....

....

....

Are there any optional commitments you've made that drain your energy? If so, what are they?

....

....

....

....

What would a smooth day look and feel like for you?

....

....

....

....

What recurring obstacles prevent smooth days from happening?

....

....

....

....

What times of day do you get distracted or procrastinate? How do you whittle that time away, and what would you rather do with it?

....

....

....

....

In the past, how have you successfully reclaimed bits of time that boosted your productivity or mood?

....

....

....

....

Who do you know who manages their time well, and what tricks or tools do they use? There's no harm in asking.

....
....
....
....

If you gave yourself ten free minutes in your day, what would you do with them?

....
....
....
....

What is the one specific aspect of your daily routine that you're most interested in changing?

....
....
....
....

SLEEP

Are you getting enough sleep? (Circle one)
YES   NO

If not, do you have trouble falling asleep, staying asleep, waking up too early, making enough time, or something else?

....
....
....
....

What is stopping you from sleeping? Are the challenges external (work/family/schedule), internal (anxiety/creative energy/physical pain), or both?

....
....
....
....

What are some ways you've considered to manage or reduce those challenges?

....
....
....
....

What is the temperature of your bedroom? (For what it's worth, research says 60 to 67 degrees Fahrenheit is ideal, and that if you're cold, wearing socks can evidently work wonders to regulate body temperature.[30])

....

What sources of light or sound might be disturbing your sleep?

....
....
....

How does physical movement during the day or before bed make a difference in your ability to sleep?

....

....

....

....

How does your mattress or pillow impact your sleep? What changes could you make to the physical setup of your bed or room?

....

....

....

....

If you could sleep any hours you wanted, what time would you fall asleep and wake up?

....

....

....

....

If that "ideal" sleep schedule is not possible due to logistics, what nightly rituals have you tried to nudge your internal clock toward the window of time you do have?

....

....

....

....

What is one approach you'd like to try next?

....

....

....

....

FOOD

How do you feel about food? What role does it play in your life?

....
....
....
....

What triggers (situations, times of day, people) bring on eating habits you don't like?

....
....
....
....

How does that impact the way you feel physically or emotionally?

....
....
....
....

What foods do you like that also make you feel sick or weighed down? And what are those symptoms like?

....
....
....
....

What foods do you enjoy that make you feel energetic and light on your feet? And how do you currently work them into your diet?

....

....

....

....

What are some other ways you could include those foods more often?

....

....

....

....

How does food impact your relationships?

....

....

....

....

List a few words to describe how it would feel to live one whole day without worrying about your diet.

....

....

....

....

How do you feel about cooking, and what are some ways to make mealtimes easier?

....

....

....

....

How do you feel about grocery shopping? What information do you need, or what apps could you use, to make it easier?

....

....

....

....

Ask a friend or family member for their favorite resource for healthy, easy recipes. (Or if you hate to cook, ask for restaurants or meal prep services that make their lives easier.)

....

....

....

....

What are a few simple ways you could dose your body with more nourishing food on a regular basis?

....

....

....

....

FITNESS

What is your definition of being fit, and is "fitness" important to you?

....
....
....
....

What kind of exercise do you do and how often?

....
....
....
....

If you're exercising already, why? What do you get out of it?

....
....
....
....

If you want to get more exercise, what do you hope it will do for you?

....
....
....
....

How have you tried to get fit in the past? Which activities felt good and which felt painful or annoying?

If you stopped exercising, when and why? What got in the way?

What are some ways you can work around those barriers?

Describe a time when moving or exercising felt good. Where were you? Who were you with? What were you wearing? What specifically felt good about it?

What are some activities you already do that involve moving but wouldn't necessarily be considered exercise? (These can be any activities that get you up on your feet: gardening, walking the dog, standing at a desk, pacing, cleaning, shopping. Every time you stand up and move, you are doing something good for your health.)

....

....

....

....

What is one new kind of movement you've been curious to try?

....

What has prevented you from trying it?

....

....

....

....

What first step could you take toward trying this new activity?

....

....

SPACE

Which of your home and work spaces, if any, feel inspiring?

....

....

....

....

Which ones make you feel grounded or comfortable?

....

....

....

....

What are your favorite colors, and where are they in your spaces?

....

....

....

....

Which rooms or locations don't feel good?

....

....

....

....

What projects, of any size, big or small, are you hoping to take on in these areas?

....
....
....
....

Which one seems most important? And why?

....
....
....
....

What feels wrong about that space, and what can be done (easily or inexpensively) to make it feel better? (New paint? New pillows? Curtains? Photos of your favorite people? Better lighting? Furniture?)

....
....
....
....

What outdoor spaces do you have access to, and how often do you give yourself time to spend there?

....
....
....
....

How much natural light do you get (indoors or out), and, if needed, how can you get more?

....
....
....
....

Whose space do you admire, and what do you like about it?

....
....
....
....

What is one easy fix or enhancement you could make to one of your spaces that would take fewer than 15 minutes?

....

What is one daily routine that would make being in your space more enjoyable?

....

PLAY

What do you like to do for fun, with no agenda other than a good time?

....

....

....

....

How often do you set aside time for hobbies, day trips, or creative pursuits that have nothing to do with work?

....

....

....

....

What prevents you from stepping away from your regular obligations?

....

....

....

....

How could one of those factors be managed to give you more flexibility?

....

....

....

....

Describe adventures or playful activities you have enjoyed regularly—during any period of your life, even if you haven't done them in ages.

....

....

....

....

Who makes you feel carefree or mischievous?

....

....

....

....

What is one fun activity that you would like to do more often?

....

What activity would you like to try for the first time?

....

What is a long-term adventure you want to have someday? Unleashed, where would you go or what would you do?

....

....

....

....

What is a mini-version of that adventure that you could do sooner?

....

....

....

....

What about restful downtime? How often are you able to read or daydream or wander, and what does that look like for you?

....

....

....

....

What benefits do you get from taking time out to relax or play?

....

....

....

....

What is one playful thing you can do in the upcoming week that doesn't require too much time or money?

....

PEOPLE

Who are your go-to people? Who allows you to feel like yourself with no pretense or effort?

....

....

....

....

How often, and in what ways, do you connect with each of those people?

....

....

....

....

How does seeing or talking with those people impact your life in other areas?

....

....

....

....

What is a small thing you can do to let one of them know you're thinking of them?

....

Who would you like to connect with more, but you haven't made the effort? What do you like about that person?

....

....

....

....

What is preventing you from growing that relationship?

....

....

....

....

What are some ways you could better connect with that person?

....

....

....

....

Who is toxic to your well-being?

....

How can time with that person be reduced so they impact your life as little as possible?

....

....

....

....

What are some ways you can set boundaries or rebound when they hurt you or piss you off?

....

....

....

....

What about animals? What other living creatures give you joy?

....

....

....

....

If you could change one thing about the relationships in your life, what would it be?

....

....

....

....

MONEY

Which of your current financial habits impact you positively?

....
....
....
....

Which ones impact you negatively?

....
....
....
....

Which one are you most interested in addressing?

....

What questions do you have about budgeting or investments?

....
....
....
....

Who could help you find answers to those questions?

....
....
....
....

What other resources (blogs, websites, apps) could you explore to find additional information about money or budgeting?

....
....
....
....

What money management tools do you have in place, or would you like to put in place, to help increase your confidence or stability?

....
....
....
....

How do you feel about your work and continuing on that career path?

....
....
....
....

If work is making you unhappy, what could be changed in your schedule, position, or chain of command to make it better?

....
....
....
....

If you're thinking of an exit strategy, what could that look like? (Allow your mind to wander on this. No one is watching. This is just an initial brainstorm.)

....
....
....
....

What is your dream career, and how might it—or something *related* to it—be attainable?

....
....
....
....

Are you satisfied with your education? And, if not, what would be your first steps to find out about continuing education?

....

....

....

....

Who can you talk to who is currently working in the field you're interested in?

....

....

What additional skills do you need to grow or change your career?

....

....

....

....

Aside from getting a raise or changing jobs, what is one way you would feel more secure financially?

....

....

....

....

SPIRIT

Are you generally aware of when your head or heart needs more attention?

....

If so, how do those messages show up in your body and mind?

....

....

....

If not, consider a time when you were highly stressed or disconnected, and describe any physical symptoms you experienced.

....

....

....

....

What does *spirit* or *spiritual connection* mean to you?

....

....

....

....

Is it important? Why or why not?

....

....

....

....

Who do you know that has a spiritual practice you're curious to learn more about?

....

....

....

....

When, where, or how do you connect with something outside of your inner monologue? (Do you go to a place of worship? Get out in nature? Meditate or do yoga? Volunteer with a group that means something to you? Create something? Other ways?)

....

....

....

....

What are a few ways you could contribute to your spiritual well-being in ten minutes or fewer?

....

....

....

....

Helping others has been shown to improve health outcomes for the helper (less stress, greater connection, physical activity, and even skill-building).[31] What are some ways you could nurture your own spirit by offering someone else time and space to nurture theirs?

....

....

....

....

VOICE

On a scale of 1 to 10, how free do you feel to speak your mind in each of the following scenarios?

▋	At work?
▋	To your partner?
▋	In bed?
▋	With neighbors?
▋	With your parents?
▋	With your children?
▋	To your best friend?
▋	To someone you don't like?
▋	In an organization you're involved with (school, religious, volunteer, etc.)?

In one of those scenarios that stands out, what prevents you from speaking your mind?

What would you say in that situation if you could speak freely?

....

....

....

....

What is the worst that could happen if you spoke up?

....

....

....

....

What is the best that could happen?

....

....

....

....

How would it feel to cut loose and let some truth fly, even if you didn't get everything you asked for?

....

....

....

....

Who inspires you with their ability to be present and truthful? Why do they stand out in your mind?

....

....

....

....

Where or with whom are you most comfortable being yourself?

....

....

....

....

How have you constrained your voice, body, or creativity in ways that no longer serve you?

....

....

....

....

What is worth speaking up for in your life right now?

....

....

....

....

How do you explore or exercise your voice, even if it is in private? (Just because you write a letter, doesn't mean you have to send it. Just because you paint a picture, doesn't mean you have to share it.)

....

....

....

....

Chapter 8

Microdosing Habits Action Plan

That was a lot of data—interesting, but a lot to process nonetheless.

Your library is officially a mess. Books are strewn everywhere, and you're sitting on the floor in the middle of it all, unsure how to process the onslaught of information. You've done extensive research into your knowledge base, but there is no way to act on any of it until you get some order in here. You can't even see the door anymore. It's over on that far wall, with the clock above it. But the books are piled so high, the exit is completely obscured. You're boxed in, and there's only one way out.

Not to worry. The next step is simple. You know what inspires you, what stops your momentum, and how it all lands in your body, for better or worse. You know what comes naturally to maintain your equilibrium. You've explored the obstacles and resources in the Ten Areas of your life.

The next step is to sort the information into piles, so you can focus on the areas calling out to you like kids shouting into an echo chamber: *Hey! Hey! Look at me! Me! Me!* This is where you get to prioritize. It's your chance to figure out what your goals are—and which habits are going to be most impactful and realistic to hit those goals.

With all of that wisdom swirling in your head, sort the Ten Areas into three piles, based on your responses on pages 94–121. Assign each to one of the following three lists:

1. The Everything Is Groovy List

2. The I Can't Deal with This Now List

3. The Hell Yeah, Let's Do It List

The Everything Is Groovy List identifies the areas that are working pretty well already. Thumbs up. Set that list aside.

The I Can't Deal with This Now List consolidates the areas that are too hard or confusing to address—or that you simply don't care enough about to bother changing. Set that list aside as well with no apologies. You can deal with it later if you're so inclined.

The Hell Yeah, Let's Do It List should contain *only one or two areas* where you are out of whack and looking for something different. **Warning**: If you put more than one or two things on this list, you will fall through a trapdoor in the floor and be consumed by the dragons below, so don't even think about it. Did I not mention the dragons before? Yeah . . . you don't want to mess with them.

Here are the categories: Time, Sleep, Food, Fitness, Space, Play, People, Money, Spirit, and Voice.

Ready, set, go.

Everything Is Groovy	I Can't Deal with This Now	Hell Yeah, Let's Do It
....	....	....
....	....	....
....	....	
....	....	
....	....	
....	....	

Excellent! Now you get to completely disregard everything except the *one* or *two* areas in Hell Yeah, Let's Do It. Are you still with us, or did I lose you to the fire-breathing beasts of the underworld? Great! Moving on.

Presto-Chango Switcheroo

In your research, you discovered empirical evidence to support two key findings regarding your past attempts (and occasional failures) to change.

First, you learned that you are not alone in the struggle to change habits you no longer want.

In *The Willpower Instinct*, Stanford University health psychologist Kelly McGonigal writes, "The science of willpower makes clear that everyone struggles in some way with temptations, addiction, distraction, and procrastination. These are not individual weaknesses that reveal our personal inadequacies. They are universal experiences and part of the human condition."[32]

Everyone, as in *everyone*, suffers from these afflictions—not everyone-except-for-you-because-you're-supposed-to-be-immune-from-transgression. You are just a human being, trying to keep it together like everyone else. So that's good to know. (You can take off the shroud of guilt you've wrapped around yourself in recent years and throw it in the nearest river now. You're not a failure; you're just human. Time to let it go.)

You've established that you are not walking around with a fatal flaw and we're all dealing with similar challenges in one way or another. Hooray! That takes a load off, but so what? Change is still elusive, and you have no idea how to achieve it.

Dr. McGonigal offers insight about how to move forward, writing: "If there is a secret for greater self-control, the science points to one thing: the power of paying attention. It's training the mind to recognize when you're making a choice, rather than running on autopilot."

So, basically, we need to snap out of it—wake up when the old impulse hits and have a new routine at the ready. If we're functioning purely on impulse and don't stop to recognize that we're even making a choice, we have no chance of making a different one.

Creating change is a practice, and that practice can be supported or sabotaged by any of the ten aspects of life you've been looking at. That's a lot of tools at your disposal and, simultaneously, a lot to juggle—but this is an abundance of useful information in your capable hands. (Clearly you are a connoisseur of great nonfiction literature.)

You're on the right track, but what does that practice need to look like? If paying attention is the key, what are you supposed to be paying attention *to*?

This leads to your second big discovery: understanding how habits work makes them a whole lot easier to change.

You find the blueprint you need in *The Power of Habit* by Charles Duhigg, a seminal book on behavioral psychology. Duhigg is an investigative reporter for the *New York Times* and winner of a whole bunch of fancy journalism awards: National Academies of Sciences, National Journalism, and George Polk awards. He won a Pulitzer Prize, too. He's a consummate journalist, but he doesn't exhaust you with a bunch of dry, epidemiological research. His book reads like a pop culture bible on the science of habit change.[33]

In it, he explains the "habit loop," a concept based on research from MIT, the University of California-San Diego, the University of North Texas, and Yale, among others. These loops form in our brains to take the strain off the day-to-day workings of our minds, so we don't have to think so hard about what to do next. If we know that 6:00 p.m. means takeout and TV, we don't have to expend any energy figuring out what to do after work each night. Fewer choices equal less drama and additional energy for more challenging tasks.

Our brains forge powerful neural pathways to make these daily decisions easier, less taxing, and more routine whenever possible. The habit loop is useful to solidify healthy habits like brushing our teeth, driving with a seat belt on, or walking after lunch, but it poses a problem when we go on autopilot with habits that aren't so helpful: skipping workouts, eating when we're not hungry, or staying up too late watching Netflix.

But our brains are just trying to help us survive. Living takes a lot of brainpower, and fewer decisions make it easier. According to *Inc.* magazine, "The average person makes 35,000 decisions every day. What to eat for breakfast? What shirt to wear? Which door to go through? Where to go for lunch? A simple way to save brainpower is to cut down on the number of decisions you need to make. Some of the most successful people have already figured this out."[34] Entrepreneurs like Dr. Dre, Steve Jobs, and Mark Zuckerberg have been famous for wearing the same thing day after day, to alleviate decision fatigue and make room for more urgent matters.

Author James Clear expands on this idea in his book, *Atomic Habits*. He writes, "When scientists analyze people who appear to have tremendous self-control, it turns out those individuals aren't all that different from those who are struggling. Instead, 'disciplined' people are better at structuring their lives in a way that does not require heroic willpower and self-control."[35]

So where does that structure begin?

The habit loop is a three-part process. It begins with a CUE or trigger—recurring exposure to a particular situation, place, person, or time of day. This trigger can be associated with stress or it can simply be a matter of daily rhythm. The cue is followed by a ROUTINE, like eating chips after dinner or scrolling through Instagram before bed. And finally, the REWARD. This can be a diversion, a boost of energy, comfort, familiarity, a rush of feel-good serotonin, sugar high, or some other payoff that tells your brain it's worth revisiting this loop tomorrow. And the day after that, too.

Three steps: cue—routine—reward.

"Habits aren't destiny," Duhigg writes. "Understanding how habits work—learning the structure of the habit loop—makes them easier to control. Once you break a habit into its components, you can fiddle with the gears."

But fiddling with the gears requires paying attention, and paying attention is hard when we're distracted, stressed, or overwhelmed, which is pretty much most of the time. Even more disturbing, research shows that once a habit is formed, it's always there. Our brains are wired to remember—forever—how to function efficiently based on the rewards that have provided us with waves of relief in the past. This means we don't forget that brushing our teeth makes our mouths feel less skanky in the morning. But it also means it's tough to forget that when we feel like a chewed-up piece of gum on the bottom of somebody else's shoe, cookie dough ice cream (or booze) makes us feel a whole lot "better."

According to researchers at MIT, whether we like it or not, our brains remember *all* the habits—all the ways of coping, "good" or "bad"—that have ever supplied us with a reliable reward.[36] Once a habit is formed, we can't forget that response completely, but we can interrupt and replace it with something else.[37] We can pull a switcheroo on the pattern by replacing the ROUTINE part of the loop. The more frequently we replace the ROUTINE and achieve a similar or equally satisfying REWARD, the more likely we are to follow the new, healthy habit and the less likely we are to lean on the old one.

Then, the brain can go offline again, and autopilot becomes much more productive. Presto-chango, you've got yourself a new healthy habit. But to get there, you have to *pay attention* to the cue and be prepared to make alternate choices in response. It's cumbersome at first. Replacing an entrenched routine definitely requires effort, and it certainly doesn't always work. Sometimes when you're trying to change a habit, you'll feel more like Scooby-Doo on ice skates than Michelle Kwan, but that's just part of the trip. You win some, you lose some. You can try again tomorrow with another approach. As Thomas Edison once said, "I have not failed. I've just found ten thousand ways that won't work."[38]

Every attempt is an exercise in not taking your choice for granted. Regardless of the outcome, if you are able to *notice* what you're doing while you're doing it, you win. You have brought the habit out of the far reaches of your unconscious and into your conscious mind.

Go Micro or Go Home

Microdoses of nourishing, pleasurable habits spread through the other areas of your life like rainbows at a Dolly Parton concert. The better you feel, and the less stressed you are, the easier making healthy choices becomes. The challenge is to keep your new habits limited, in both scope and number, at the beginning so they don't collapse in on themselves. These tiny changes can seem negligible, but when you achieve them, you gain something even more significant than the change itself. You build confidence, and when you have confidence, bigger changes follow.

On the other hand, when you set a big, unwieldy goal and are unable to achieve it, you break a promise to yourself. It's a betrayal, a breach of your own trust. You lose faith in your ability to follow through next time—and that leads to a spin cycle of guilt and self-doubt. (If you're going to go that route, you might as well dive back in the river and pull out that old shroud of guilt. It's sopping wet and heavy now, but you can carry it around a while longer if you like.)

Micro-sized habit changes make problems more manageable and goals more attainable. You can do this anytime, anywhere for the low, low cost of totally free. There are no barriers to entry.

Go small or go home. I'll say it again: it's a practice.

Our bodies and minds are not clear-cut. They're a bit squirmy, in fact. They're hard to nail down—perpetual experiments with no final solutions, only theories to investigate.

The *Oxford English Dictionary* defines the scientific method as "a method of . . . systematic observation, measurement, and experimentation—the formulation, testing, and modification of hypotheses."[39]

Modification of hypotheses. That phrase makes me horny.

We are creatures in flux, forever growing. We are never stuck. There is always an opportunity for growth, and when we approach change with a spirit of observation and experimentation, we are able to progress—or, at least, have some fun. Consider each attempt at change to be a little research and development for your body house—R&D on a micro-scale.

If you beat yourself up every time you try something new and it doesn't work out, you'll collapse under the weight of frustration. But if you chalk it up to a learning experience, you can add that "failure" to the list of ideas that did not turn out to be useful, check it off the list, and move on to the next. It's a process of trial and error, not a personal failing.

Two Types of Habits

There is room on the following pages to work through two types of habits: Replacement Habits and Additional Habits. Both are important, but, to start, focusing on just one may be your best bet. Decision fatigue is real. Our brains can take on only so many projects at once. Old routines are entrenched, and distractions are plentiful. So it's best to reduce effort whenever possible. As Duhigg writes, ". . . habits allow our minds to ramp down more often. This effort-saving instinct is a huge advantage. An efficient brain requires less room . . . [It] allows us to stop thinking constantly about basic behaviors, such as walking and choosing what to eat, so we can devote mental energy to inventing spears, irrigation systems, and, eventually airplanes and video games."

Presumably, you have an irrigation system to invent somewhere or an empire to build. Your new habits will support these endeavors. But while the habits are still unfamiliar, they will take up some of that mental stamina. Staying actively engaged with a new choice is labor-intensive, so if one change feels better than two, stick with one.

I offer two options because sometimes people discover that coming at a single problem from two directions can be useful. For instance, if you have insomnia, quitting caffeine after noon and stretching for five minutes before bed could both contribute significantly to solving the problem . . . which means you see a quicker payoff and get more sleep . . . which means you'll have more energy to make additional changes like exercising . . . which helps you sleep better again . . . which focuses your mind at work . . . which gets you a raise . . . which increases your confidence . . . which gets you a date . . . which improves your sex life . . . which helps you sleep even better . . . and off you go, cartwheeling through fields of daisies.

Quitting caffeine in the afternoon requires a Replacement Habit, a substitute that offers a similar reward to what you get from drinking coffee: something to give you energy (a walk, a stretch, fresh air); something to warm or comfort you while you work (music, decaf, herbal tea, or a scarf); social interaction (a break room meet-up or walk with a coworker). Once you know what you're getting out of the habit, you can figure out your own unique ways to fill that need.

Stretching for five minutes before bed, on the other hand, is an Additional Habit. You're not trying to quit anything here. You're just adding something new that makes one of your Ten Areas feel smoother, better, or easier. (This would become a Replacement Habit if you needed to stop some other late-night routine to make it possible.)

If you decide to aim for two changes, you can choose two of the same type or one of each—but it's important to know which type is which. Replacement Habits are more common than Additional ones. When we implement something new, we are frequently (but not always) replacing something old. No habitual behavior should ever be cut out without an alternative to fill the void by delivering a nice cozy, nurturing buzz. You will find a set of questions on the coming pages to help you experiment, but one habit at a time is more than enough.

Either way, the linchpin for successful change is in the REWARD. As I wrote in *Lightness of Body and Mind*, "You can't get a body you love by doing things that you hate." The reward for a new routine has to be pleasurable, and it has to be quick. If the payoff takes too long to arrive or doesn't feel good, odds are you won't stick with it.

The research backs this up. A University of Chicago study, "Immediate Rewards Predict Adherence to Long-Term Goals," puts it plainly. "People primarily pursue long-term goals, such as exercising, to receive delayed rewards (e.g., improved health). However, we find that the presence of immediate rewards is a stronger predictor of persistence in goal-related activities than the presence of delayed rewards. Specifically, immediate rewards (e.g., enjoyment) predicted current persistence."[40]

It makes sense. The more pleasure you get along the way, the more likely you are to stick with it. As you answer the questions on the following pages to build new habits or replace old ones, consider the following four elements:

1. Make the new choice easy and accessible.

2. Keep it small.

3. Find ways to get immediate rewards (pleasure, comfort, connection, fun).

4. Modify as needed. Modification of hypotheses, baby!

The website Biology 4 Kids describes the scientific method as "learning how to learn."[41] Bad habits can be frustrating, but the solutions don't have to be. *Play* with your options. Learn how to learn, all over again. These initial efforts are primarily for the purpose of observation. They might work. They might not. They might change your life. They might turn out to be unimportant, or they might lead you to a far more interesting idea.

In that spirit, here is your chance to explore the possibilities.

Habit #1: The Replacement Habit

Which of the ten areas are you addressing?

....

What is the specific habit giving you grief?

....

What happens right before you do it? (Where are you? What time is it? Who is there?)

....

....

....

....

What are some ways you could avoid or reduce exposure to the trigger?

....

....

....

....

What is the first thing you notice as you're triggered, before you take action?

....

....

....

....

When the trigger hits, how can you create a pause to pay active attention to the choice you're making?

....
....
....
....

What is the immediate payoff you get from repeating this habit (before the regret kicks in)?

....
....
....
....

What alternate habit do you want to try instead?

....

Would that alternative bring a similar sense of immediate gratification? If not, what else could you try?

....
....
....
....

Write a direct statement about what you plan to do and why. (Example: Screens off at 9:00 p.m. because I want to get some sleep, so I'm not enraged by every human unfortunate enough to cross my path between 6:00 and 10:00 a.m.)

....

....

....

....

How will you keep track of how frequently you pull off this plan, and who will provide accountability to support your efforts??

....

....

....

....

Note the first time you make the new choice and how it feels, physically and emotionally.

....

....

....

....

After giving it a shot, are you still invested in this idea? Or would you rather try something else?

....

....

....

....

If you decided not to make this change, why? What got in the way or turned out not to matter?

....
....
....
....

What else might be interesting to try?

....
....
....
....

If you decide to stick with the original plan, why? What are you getting out of it?

....
....
....
....

Whether this first attempt works out, if you answer those questions, you'll be closer to achieving your goal than most people ever get. Like I said in chapter 1, this isn't advanced engineering. It's a practice of connecting with what's important to you, observing your patterns, giving yourself a break, and trying some alternatives in a systematic, supported, nonjudgmental way.

It all begins with the art of observation: *Well, look at that. Here I go again, doing that thing that feels good in the moment and crappy later. Huh. I wonder why that happens. Maybe I'll watch it a few more times to see if I can figure out what I'm craving—and if there are healthier ways to get it!*

We all have helpful and not-so-helpful ways of managing stress; the idea here is to dislodge the "bad" ones by drowning them in good ones.

Every time that trigger arrives, you get a chance to choose whether to go with your new response or the old one. Your prefrontal cortex (the part of the brain that makes conscious decisions) might be offline sometimes (or lots of times)—off on a tangent, wondering about those dragons again. *Did she say dragons?!* You may have to go through the old cycle a few more times (or a few hundred), but eventually—if you give yourself options; your goals are connected to What Matters; and you've built in some kind of quick reward—you're going to feel an authentic urge to try the new thing.

If you're successful in recognizing the CUE and making a different choice, even once or twice, you are signaling to your reptilian brain that you are capable, invested, and getting a benefit. Over time, as you repeat the new behavior, the structure of the neural pathways in your brain will begin to change, exponentially multiplying your odds of long-term success—especially if you can persist through the initial, inevitable brushes with "failure." According to the *British Journal of General Practice*, a publication that brings research into clinical practice, habit-formation begins with an "initiation phase," develops through a "learning phase," and "culminates in the 'stability phase', at which the habit has formed and its strength has plateaued, so that it persists over time with minimal effort or deliberation."[42] If your habits don't work out right off the bat, it doesn't mean you're tragically flawed. You're just establishing patterns and figuring out what works.

(I can tell you, from personal experience, that listening to a political podcast does not provide the same midnight stress relief as eating a bowl of cereal—and neither leads to a good night's sleep. A bath and a book, on the other hand, have a fighting shot at quieting the nocturnal voices in my head. Still sorting this one out.)

Truth: If you want to keep going through successes and failures alike, all the good juju lives in the REWARD. *Feed it.* What are you aching for? Is it rest? Relief? More energy? Companionship? Distraction? Stress reduction?

Recognize the trigger, replace the routine, and keep the reward.

If this first change doesn't turn out to be the right one (not important enough or too difficult), keep looking for other options. You'll find something that works better eventually, if you stay in the game. The more you play with this process, the easier it gets. Forward ho. On to the next.

If the thought of quitting *anything* is too hard—a reasonable concern, considering how many of us "fail" to quit various habits on a daily basis—you might prefer to *start* doing something new, rather than stopping (and replacing) something old. The next questions can help you implement a new routine without worrying about deprivation or loss.

Habit #2: The Additional Habit

Which of the Ten Areas are you addressing?

....

What is one new, reinforcing habit that you want to create in that area?

....

Why do you want to add this habit?

....

....

....

....

What immediate gratification would you get out of it?

....

....

What long-term benefits do you expect to gain from it?

....

....

....

....

When and how do you plan to implement it?

....

....

....

....

What supplies or preparations could make it easier to implement?

....

....

....

....

What are some ways you could link it to an existing habit that already comes automatically to you? (Examples: Doing a thirty-second plank before brushing your teeth. Meditating for three minutes while brewing your morning coffee. Inviting a friend to lunch on Tuesdays. Taking a multivitamin with dinner.)

....

....

....

....

Write a direct statement about what you plan to do: when, how, and why.

How will you track how frequently you follow through, and create some accountability?

Note the first time you make the new choice and how it feels physically and emotionally.

After trying it out, do you still like this plan, or would you rather try something else?

If you decide not to make this change, why not? What got in the way or turned out not to matter?

....
....
....
....

What would you like to try instead?

....
....
....
....

If you decide to stick with the original plan, why? What do you like about it?

....
....
....
....

The Velvet Chair

You did it. You sorted through the mess. The path to the door is clear. The books are back in their proper places, categorized and ready for the next time you get the urge for some *modification of hypotheses*, you naughty, spicy thing. You'll know right where everything is the next time you go on a research rampage. *Meow.*

But before you go, have a seat in the comfy velvet chair in the corner, rest, and take in all your great work. Switch on the table lamp, and see if you can remember What Matters and What You're Good At. Write down the key words you selected in chapters 3 and 4 (pages 53 and 61), one more time (or update them if needed). The changes you're making are only useful if they're connected to what's important, and they'll only come to be if you use your strengths to help them grow.

What Matters

- ....
- ....
- ....

What You're Good At

- ....
- ....
- ....

Right here in the chair, in this beautiful light, surrounded by the wisdom of the ages printed in volumes from floor to ceiling, you are clear. You know where you're headed and what you need to do. You understand how and why your old habits were imprinted on your brain and how to begin forging new ones. You are confident in your capacity for change, but realistic and full of grace for the inevitable process of trial and error that awaits. You take a breath and push down on the arms of the chair as you stand to leave. The chair groans beneath your weight. "Don't forget," it says.

Say what? Did that chair just talk to you, or are you finally losing your mind?

You sit down and stand back up again.

"Don't forget."

Okay, you think. *I'll bite.* "Don't forget what?"

Sitting in that easy chair, you have all the knowledge you need. But it would be awfully cumbersome to strap a giant chair to your back and lug it around everywhere you go. No, you'll have to remember, as best you can, what changes you're making and *why*—and come back to sit a spell as needed.

It's lovely to make these goals here in the library with your philosopher hat on. But it's all too easy to stand up and walk out, put this book down, drift back into life, and forget all about it, New Year's Resolution—style.

Perhaps a reminder is in order.

It helps to set a date to come back and check in—a week or a month from now—to have a seat, back in the velvet chair, and see how it all went. *Don't forget.*

Consider putting a date on your calendar to come back to this page and note what's changed or what hasn't, how it feels, if any of this is proving useful, if habits need to be updated or altered, or if your priorities have shifted. There is no failure, only greater insight. Set the date. This chair and your library will be waiting, judgment-free.

The dragons will be there too, lingering patiently, waiting for you to slip up by fixating on too many goals rather than luxuriating in one or two. And they are definitely judging you, so don't give them the satisfaction.

Habit #1 Follow-Up

Date:

Observations:

Habit #2 Follow-Up

Date:

Observations:

One Small Stone

S tepping out of the library and out of the house, you discover a beautiful, covered bridge, with ivy growing up and over the sides, permanently connecting the front porch to your Liquid Brick Road. Beneath it runs a stream of melted snow, making its way from the mountains around your house, down to the lake and, eventually, to the Town of Favorite Things. You can cross that bridge and go exploring any time you like with no worry of getting lost. The road always leads back home—but never in ways you expect.

At the base of the bridge, you pick up a small stone, weathered and smoothed over by the elements. You can put this stone in your pocket if you want, as a symbol of stability, all things familiar. But when you're ready—if you feel like uprooting a little something, changing the status quo just slightly with an incendiary little change: a fresh haircut, a desktop purge, a stretch break in a marathon meeting, or a new houseplant—hurl that stone as hard as you can and watch it skip away. There are thousands of stones at the base of that bridge.

It's just a rock, after all, a little piece of the past you're ready to do without.

Many inspired creations begin with a shift of the status quo. Micro-changes have a way of multiplying.

If you could make one small, external change in your surroundings or routine to light a spark, what would it be?

....

And what's stopping you?

....

....

....

....

Chapter 9

Emergency Plan

The habit changes you chose in the last chapter are built around you and your needs. You have crafted them to improve your quality of life—to catapult you out of your rut and into whatever is around the bend. They are changes for the best of times, when you are settled safely at home and have your wits about you.

But what happens when everything falls apart? A loved one dies. A medical diagnosis or injury derails you. You lose your job. Your nightmare political candidate wins the race. Your heart gets broken. You've lost your footing entirely, and you're in free fall.

Suddenly every area of well-being gets shifted to the I Can't Deal with This Now List. Your best intentions fall by the wayside, and all your progress slips. This is when you need your Emergency Plan, your *I'm so blindsided I can't see straight and I'm barely keeping my head above water* plan.

Demons begin crawling out of the trees and bushes around your house. You make a run for the front door, but the way is blocked by a fanged creature limping menacingly in your direction with one septic, malformed leg dragging behind. You turn to cross the bridge instead and are ambushed by an army of winged beasts, with sharp talons and vacant eyes, swooping overhead.

You take cover in the garage, grateful that the unwieldy mechanical door still works. It rises just in time. You dive into the relative safety of the orb and push off, in search of a remedy to rid your house of these monsters from the abyss.

When all else fails, the orb is home base.

Free Fall

Tumbling frantically, head over feet, you realize now is the time to summon all the insights you gathered on your travels. This is your opportunity to build the platform and handrails that will keep you stable when you hit nauseatingly rough terrain.

We will be brief, as there is no time to waste in emergency circumstances such as this.

Each reinforcement you build in the orb is a part of your safety zone. When the world is spinning too fast, all you have to do is plant your feet or grab on. No thinking required.

These supports are crucial for lasting progress. They prevent you from collapsing under the weight of unexpected crises, and they sustain you through daily indignities that feel like death by a thousand cuts. They hold you up like a frenzied crowd at a stadium show. When all is lost, you can throw your head back and surf your way to the safety of the stage.

Without them, you'd crash from one side of the orb to the other in a bid to outrun the monsters—slip, break a rib, lose your ability to breathe, and forget yourself entirely in the fight for survival.

With this system in place, you'll still go for a hell of a ride, but you will find visitations from the netherworld much less daunting—and recovery easier—so you can get back to What Matters, back to your tiny, transformative changes.

The reinforcements consist of the following: **three people, three places, three kinds of physical activity, three foods**, and **three works of art** (music, visual, or otherwise) that ground you and remind you that being alive is strange and beautiful—even as it breaks your heart, and sometimes your body, too.

Who offers you peace of mind? What places drop your shoulders and slow your breathing? What physical activities calm or focus you? Which foods give you energy or comfort? And what songs, movies, or works of art restore your spirit?

The **people** are the platform beneath your feet.

The **places** are the padding that shields your head when you land upside down.

The **physical activities** and **foods** are handrails to help you stay upright and aligned.

And the **works of art** are glimmers of light that make this part of the journey bearable.

This is your go-to survival guide when all hell breaks loose. It's hard to remember anything at all when you're grieving or in shock—much less how to take care of yourself so you don't take ten steps back. Dog-ear this page and turn to it any time you forget how to breathe. Pick something on your list, and hang on for dear life. It will get you through until the world stops spinning.

The items on this list should not be difficult to identify, but if you need help, refer back to what you found in your Town of Favorite Things (page 72).

Honey's words echo in your head. "Every reinforcement must be chosen for the love of it," she said. "Your Favorite Things bring you peace, connection, or excitement. They give you life."

Your body knows what soothes your spirit and eases your pain—and what doesn't. The following list is a collection of reliable, easy-access remedies for hard times, busy times, all the times. It's a go-to source of relief.

EMERGENCY REINFORCEMENTS

People

1. ....
2. ....
3. ....

Places

1. ....
2. ....
3. ....

Physical Activities

1. ....
2. ....
3. ....

Foods

1. ....
2. ....
3. ....

Art

1. ....
2. ....
3. ....

You're cruising now. The monsters batted you around for a while, but the orb kept rolling back to center, back to the intersection at the base of the driveway. That brand of persistent resilience is no fun for the monsters. They couldn't get to you, so they've given up and moved on to someone else's house, someone else's intersection, someone less prepared to roll with the punches.

You haven't eradicated stress, but you have made it infinitely more manageable. From now on, you will recognize it when it arrives—whether it appears in the form of demons or heavy fog. You'll see it for what it is, knowing full well that it will pass. Odds are it won't kill you, at least not yet. In the meantime, you've got your people, your places, ways of moving and feeding your body, your artwork, and your favorite music cranked up to ten. You'll hunker down in the orb and step out again when the danger recedes—to take your rightful place back in your house, stronger than ever. Ready for whatever comes next.

PART III

The Payoff

Chapter 10

Power

R eturning home, you are shaken but not stirred.

In fact, you're remarkably unfazed. You know how to do this now. You're capable of progress when life is stable and resilient when the monsters come out to play.

You're feeling quite pliable: stretchy, limber, and lithe. You're like Elastigirl from *The Incredibles*, able to reach remarkable distances and shape-shift to adapt to whatever challenges come your way. It's beginning to feel like a superpower.

You stand in front of your body house, assessing the state of things, and decide it's time for a facelift. The peeling paint on the front door is vexing. It's faded, cracked, and no longer represents who you are or how you feel.

If you remember correctly, there are cans of paint in the attic, an array of colors to choose from, and you'd like to have a look. Feet planted in place, you begin to stretch through your torso, legs, and arms. Up you go, past the first floor.

At two stories tall, you peek in the window beneath the eaves. There's a lot of stuff up there, long since forgotten. Photo albums, boxes of illicit notes passed in middle school study hall, vestiges of family lore, and journals written earnestly by younger configurations of yourself.

You wonder why everything in life seems so important at the time but—before you know it—ends up buried in a box in a dusty attic, replaced by a new round of concerns. You try to remember how you accumulated so much stuff. Whatever is up there, you know you probably don't want most of it anymore, moth-eaten artifacts from bygone eras. And the things you do want would be better served by purging the clutter. You're no longer interested in harboring every feeling and indulging every dubious rumination. The attic is messy, and you're over it.

You decide you're not going to be able to get anything done on the outside until you clear out the inside to see what's in your way. How hard could it be? All you have to do is figure out what's worth keeping and what needs to go in the junk bin.

Your stretchy skills will come in handy here: you won't even have to schlep up and down the stairs to clear out the piles of trash. This project would be straightforward . . . if only you could get that window open! But it appears to be stuck. It's rusted or painted or rotted shut.

SPROING. Back to normal size, you head over to the pile of rocks at the base of the bridge. There must be one big enough to break some glass. No time for subtleties. No time for chisels. You're in the mood to break some shit.

You find a rock about the size of your head. *That'll do.* Up you go again, stretching to the top of the house, and hurling that small boulder through the window with a wave of fresh air blowing in behind it. Brilliant. Now you have easy access. You lay an old tarp over what remains of the glass and lean your body through the window. Feet on the ground, head and arms in the attic, you thumb through LPs and brush mouse droppings off a duffle bag filled with perma-stained sheets from your first-ever apartment. At the time, they weren't quite bad enough to toss but were too gross to use—and here they sit.

You're faced with a decision. Keep the stuff piled in the attic or discard it all except the things that feel like home—physical representations of who you are and who you want to be going forward. You could just push aside the junk and look for the paint, but now that you know this clutter is there, ignoring it feels like you've got a fifty-pound rucksack strapped to your back. There's no room for it anymore. As Marie Kondo chirped in *The Life-Changing Magic of Tidying Up*, "The question of what you want to own is actually the question of how you want to live your life."[43]

What do you want to own? And we're not talking about wardrobe here.

You've done a huge amount of work on this journey. By doing so, you have asserted jurisdiction over your life. You are making room for the things you care about by tossing the routines you have transcended. You're feeling buoyant. Your back is strong, and your heart is beating steadily. You know now that the contributions you make—at work, at home, and in the world—are amplified when you clear every bit of clutter you can spare. It starts right here in the attic with old stories you've told yourself about who you're supposed to be and what you can or cannot do—archaic patterns and beliefs you can choose to keep or discard.

Stuff. Too much stuff.

You began this book with a vision for the changes you wanted to achieve. You have big picture, long-term goals. Maybe you want a view with floor-to-ceiling windows. Maybe you want to set an example for your kids. Maybe you want to spite your ex, start a business, get a master's degree, or become financially stable. Maybe you want to lose twenty pounds. Maybe you want to save the planet—ease the pain and suffering of the human race. Or maybe you just want your head to stop hurting.

By unflinchingly grasping and honoring your current location, recognizing your biggest challenges, and implementing your personal support system, you flex your muscles of personal advocacy. You confirm that you have the power to respond proactively to any challenge—and to spread that power to the people you work with, the organizations you run, the children you raise, and the network of friends you rely on. You experience personal power firsthand, which, in turn, bolsters your confidence and self-worth. You learn what you are capable of, what we are all capable of, and you'll be damned if you're not going to spread that wealth.

Jurisdiction

In 1991, an eleven-year-old girl named Marcia lost her mother, Diane—a South Korean immigrant who, at age thirty-seven, died of ovarian cancer that spread to her lungs. Marcia was left behind in St. Louis, Missouri, with her little brother and their father—a retired army officer. She isn't sure what his rank was and doesn't care to talk about what he did for a living after the army. What Marcia knows for sure, though, is that her father's priorities for her were to "look pretty and marry well." When she was sixteen, he urged her to move in with her twenty-three-year-old boyfriend who was, like her dad, dismissive and abusive.

After her mom died, Marcia steeled herself against the world. As she puts it, "I told myself, 'You cannot stay here. You need to get out, and you're going to have to do it by yourself. You've got to get your armor on.'" These were not the idle musings of a little girl. The armor was real, and the mission was nonnegotiable.

Throughout the years, Marcia took to following her gut to survive. She worked in the automotive and finance industries. She went to Parsons School of Design in New York City before putting aside her dream of becoming a fashion designer in favor of opening her own boutique in St. Louis with the help of a generous mentor. For a while, she had a radio show and managed bands on the road. She has been a grassroots organizer for PETA, a senior community manager for Yelp, and an editor at *The Tennessean*. She is currently owner and CEO of Roar Nashville,[44] a mission-driven branding, strategy, and communications firm. She also cofounded Nashville Fashion Week and founded her own charity, the Tiny but Mighty Fund, which has been promoting animal welfare for more than seven years. In short, Marcia Masulla is a badass, but her badassery has come at a cost.

At age twenty-one and again at twenty-seven, Marcia fought her own battle with ovarian cancer. She hid the impact of those treatments from her friends and employers and persevered through both diagnoses—only to face a violent series of eleven ovarian cyst ruptures over a span of sixteen months in her mid-thirties. Through every health challenge, the armor Marcia wore became simultaneously more important and more difficult to carry. Without it, she felt weak and exposed. With it, she was isolated and fatigued.

To combat that growing sense of unease, she worked herself to the bone and reaped the benefits of a diverse career built around the causes and pastimes she has always loved.

"That time in my life looked so successful," she told me, "but it created a long journey of unhealthy behaviors. I was a ridiculous workaholic. I averaged three to four hours of sleep per night for seven years. I craved hitting goals and deadlines. I got high from achievements—but had to continue to succeed more and more in order to feel valid. I benefited professionally but made tremendous sacrifices in the romantic and personal aspects of my life. I relished in my armor and believed for so long that 'vulnerability' was a filthy word, not just dirty—*filthy*—but, in recent years, I had to look at myself and realize that I had a problem. I wasn't okay."

"My goals were fulfilled," she says, "but they weren't fulfilling."

Marcia is now thirty-nine, and her armor is beginning to rust. She doesn't need it as much anymore. Lugging that protective shield around for nearly three decades strengthened her spine and steadied her resolve. It helped her survive and got her where she is today. But it's beginning to feel like dead weight now. It's weighing her down more than keeping her safe, and she is discovering how much more powerful it feels to take off the armor and walk free.

Marcia says, "I'm building better systems to take care of myself, and I'm also starting to realize that there are some things that will never be part of a system and I've got to let go . . . Even when things are scary and I don't have the answers, my intuition has never once let me down. Going forward, for me to be the best person I can be and have the most impact, I have to choose to take care of myself. I'm softer now, more connected to people, aware of how I'm spending my time, and I can feel the reverb from that.

"I still have my armor on a lot of the time. Putting it down isn't natural for me. I always thought if I didn't put 180 percent into everything I did, then it was all going to fail. But I finally realized: No, sis, you've got to make space. You've gotta make space in your life. When you do, everything is so much better."

Marcia is taking jurisdiction by making space, by clearing out what she no longer needs and making conscious choices about what qualities to keep, what ambitions to elevate, and what parts of herself still need protecting. Her priorities were obscured in the attic until now, but by making space, she can figure out which ones matter and put them where they belong.

Marcia is functioning now with a cooler, more flexible nervous system that makes space for being at ease—at least some of the time, even when life feels risky and unresolved.

She has endured more than her fair share of tragedy. She had a painful childhood and more health problems as a young woman than anyone should ever have to face, but her response to those adversities couldn't have been more normal. Our bodies protect us from harm by going into fight-flight-or-freeze mode in stressful situations. That physiological mechanism helped Marcia sustain her energy over the last twenty-eight years. She needed armor and adrenaline to get her through, but that perpetual strain took a toll on her body and, eventually, on her productivity, as well.

So many strong, smart, determined people struggle to prioritize and value their health. I've been training and coaching for seventeen years and have been on two book tours so far—and I am consistently astonished by how unaware people are of their own strength and beauty, of what a difference they make and how much their well-being matters to the rest of us. As I talk with groups and individual clients, the view I have of the people sitting across from me rarely aligns with the way they see themselves. People simply don't realize how much power is lost when they undermine and neglect themselves, often for baseless and insignificant reasons: too short, too tall, too busy, too weak, too weird. It sets my hair on fire.

We need these people. We need you. When you ignore your health until it combusts into a massive inferno, you rob yourself of jurisdiction—and you rob the rest of us of your contribution. You find yourself up in the attic with your head stuck in a laundry basket circa 1999, banging into walls and wondering why you can't seem to get anything done.

It's easy to recognize and honor your friends' strengths, as you did on page 62. *How can they not see how awesome they are?!* But your friends witness that same missed opportunity in you, that same nagging inability to let the old stories, the old reel-to-reel tapes, disintegrate to make room for new ones.

Most people's perception of themselves is obscured by the peeling paint on the front door and the clutter in the attic. (There are some who think they have their house perfectly in order, of course, but who wants to hang out with them?) Nobody's perfect, and anyone worthy of your time is on a journey of their own, bumping into their own walls with their own dusty laundry baskets over their heads.

Breath

We try to make ourselves look and feel better by accumulating more—more stuff, more technology, more money, more titles, more accolades. But the drive to achieve in order to prove our value is a trick: Fit the mold. Check the boxes. Climb the ladder. Get the job. Marry the beauty queen, and you'll be fine. Once you've achieved something, throw it in the attic and pursue something else. It keeps us busy chasing all the things while chronically overlooking the one that matters most: quality of life—for us, and for the people around us, too.

Research is conclusive: when we create work-life balance, as individuals and on a larger scale in our organizations, we benefit enormously. We reduce fatigue, anxiety, stress, blood pressure, cholesterol, weight gain, sleep and digestive problems, aches and pains, and health-care costs—and we improve memory, focus, learning, empathy, creativity, collaboration, innovation, leadership, persistence, confidence, and social and emotional intelligence.

Rest, space, and play are healing therapies and, ultimately, sources of power. They are fuel for greater well-being and productivity—but don't take my word for it.

The *New York Times* reports that at the health insurance company Aetna, employees participating in mindfulness programs "report, on average, a 28 percent reduction in their stress levels, a 20 percent improvement in sleep quality and a 19 percent reduction in pain. They also become more effective on the job, gaining an average of 62 minutes per week of productivity each, which Aetna estimates is worth $3,000 per employee per year."[45] [46]

Researchers out of the University of Illinois at Urbana-Champagne produced a study on playfulness, focused on 898 students from three universities. "Findings revealed that playful individuals reported lower levels of perceived stress than their less playful counterparts, more frequently utilized adaptive, stressor-focused coping strategies, and were less likely to employ negative, avoidant, and escape-oriented strategies . . . playfulness serves a strong adaptive function with university students, providing them with specific cognitive resources from which they can manifest effective coping behaviors in the face of stressful situations."[47]

A study by the National Institutes of Health and the *American Journal for Lifestyle Medicine* found that holistic, client-centered health coaching focused on diet and exercise interventions resulted in clinically relevant reductions of blood pressure, LDL cholesterol, triglycerides, body weight, and risk for heart disease and diabetes.[48]

A Public Library of Science meta-study, "Effects of Mindfulness-Based Stress Reduction on Employees' Mental Health," reports, "The strongest outcomes were reduced levels of emotional exhaustion (a dimension of burnout), stress, psychological distress, depression, anxiety, and occupational stress. Improvements were found in terms of mindfulness, personal accomplishment, (occupational) self-compassion, quality of sleep, and relaxation."[49]

Regarding sleep, the *Journal of Occupational and Environmental Medicine* published a study of 4,188 employees from four U.S. corporations, determining that "insomnia and insufficient sleep syndrome groups had significantly worse productivity, performance, and safety outcomes . . . [but] workplace flexibility (allowing more flexible work start and end times) may contribute to positive lifestyle behaviors, and may play an important role in effective worksite health promotion programs."[50]

And according to the *Guardian* newspaper, "Intel is moving to make a nine-week mindfulness program available to its workforce of over 100,000 employees in 63 countries across the globe [because] . . . People get more authentically related to each other—beyond competency levels and their roles. So real ideas are heard and received, and people are much more generative together. The corporate mask that people put on when they walk through the door comes down."[51]

The bigwigs know it—and that's all fine and good—but we know it, too: when we prioritize time to move and breathe and allow our minds to wander, we are happier, more fulfilled, and more creative creatures. We don't need the *New York Times* and National Institutes of Health to tell us that.

Anyone can take a deep breath, but it's easier said than done when you're in chronic pain, when you're working three jobs, or when your heart is breaking. Fortunately, there is no right or wrong way to breathe. Resting your attention on a single breath is a victory: one inhale and one exhale. Remembering to do it is the key that opens doors so you can stop banging into walls.

Breath is the beginning of power. Those in power are never afraid to take the jurisdiction to breathe.

So take a moment—anytime, anywhere you want—to claim what's yours. Close your eyes and take a breath: it belongs to you. With it, you have all the power you need to find your way out of the labyrinth in your head. Breath is the fiercest weapon you have to take agency over what you do and do not want in your life. It's a label-maker for when you're overwhelmed, up in the attic: *This belief, this assumption, this habit is worth keeping. This one is not.* Breath gives you the space to know the difference, to label it and place it where it belongs.

Impact

People—and businesses, too—spend a lot of time on defense. We respond to what comes our way. We manage. We get by. We orb downhill, spinning madly, colliding with whatever food, fitness, or fiscal plan is in our path, bouncing off each other and careening where the rebound takes us. But when we honor our breath, drop our armor, and drop our assumptions, we make room for growth. We take jurisdiction. We might try one approach and find it doesn't work, but that "failure" leads us to another breath and another avenue. There is no such thing as total control, but a little preparation, a sense of adventure, and the sweet taste of micro-success goes a long way toward changing the trajectory of a life, a company, or a cause.

So what is success? What does it mean to take that power and have an impact?

Toni Morrison said, "If you are free, you need to free somebody else. If you have some power, then your job is to empower somebody else."[52]

A client of mine named Cora offers a great example of what freeing somebody else can look like, on a microscale.[53] She has spent the last couple years working with me to rewrite her assumptions about her body and to break the cycle of deprivation and guilt she has endured around food. She battled her body for much of her adult life, grasping at diets and fitness fads, craving processed foods and then banishing them from her pantry. During her childhood, there wasn't time or money to devote to proper nutrition. "Iceberg lettuce was the primary source of vegetables in our house," she said.

Over the years, Cora has worked to change her micro-habits, one at a time, which has led her to appreciate her body and feed it more nutritious food. She drinks more water. She walks more. She eats a healthy snack now and then. She met a friend at the Y once a week for a while, until she didn't. She questioned whether her body was actually that bad—and what a "bad" body means anyway. And she decided to feed herself, instead of starving herself.

Recently, after returning from Thanksgiving at her family home in Alabama, Cora came in for a session with me. She'd been accustomed to putting on her armor during the holidays, preparing herself to "fail," and making all kinds of plans to redeem herself afterward by rationing food or exercising obsessively. But this year was different.

Cora reported that this was the first Thanksgiving it didn't even cross her mind how much she should eat, how to measure her portion sizes, or what kinds of workouts she would need to do to get her body back in shape. She just went to dinner, enjoyed the food, and enjoyed her family. This was radical for her. Not only did she eat whatever she wanted that night, she spent the rest of the weekend preparing snacks: real, fresh, unprocessed snacks that she has come to crave. Her ten-year-old nephew, a kid who lives on chips and candy bars, was watching her chop strawberries and asked if he could have some. After trying them, he asked his mom if they could start eating strawberries at their house, too. Stunned by the request, his mom agreed, and now they bring home fresh fruit every time they go grocery shopping.

Nobody had a fight. Nobody told anybody what to do. The only thing different was Cora's approach: letting Thanksgiving dinner be Thanksgiving dinner, and then bringing healthy food into the house to share, instead of condemning her relatives for eating wrong and contributing to all of her problems. By listening to her body and by giving herself some grace, she was able to offer her family an opportunity to see things in a new light.

And now her nephew is changed. And the way her sister shops is changed. And demand at the grocery store has changed. And their wholesale orders change. And the market shifts. And farmers start growing differently. And the government starts subsidizing differently (hopefully). And soil is richer, and we all live better. Okay, that's the heartland in me, but it's true. Small changes matter.

Cora did something, something important. And she's not just setting an example for her family. She's setting one for her friends, too—friends who scorn their bodies and ration calories when they go out for dinner on Saturday nights. She is changing the conversation in her community by demonstrating another option to the people she loves—and other folks too, the ones who shop at the same stores and walk the same sidewalks.

She started by listening: first to her body; then to her instincts; and then to her nephew and her friends. She moved the needle by changing her habits incrementally, and now those habits have grown beyond the bounds of her personal experience. Impact can be had at every level.

What have you accomplished in the past that you are proud of?

....

....

....

....

What do you want to contribute going forward?

....

....

....

....

What does "success" mean to you?

....

....

....

....

This practice of listening and responding goes beyond our lives as individuals. For people in policy-making positions—in government, corporations, small businesses, nonprofits, schools, or religious groups—consider what success means to you on an organizational level. If you gave a microphone to each person you manage and they could tell you what they need, in terms of quality of life, to make their work more engaging and fulfilling—the truth, with no repercussions—what would they say? What does success mean to them? And how can that combined vision grow your impact?

....

....

....

....

....

What mechanisms do you have in place to hear and respond to those messages?

....

....

....

And if you're not in a leadership position—you're simply a person in charge of being your own person—what would make quality of life better for you? What microdoses of life, love, or liberty could make it better? This can be anything at all that you have jurisdiction to change.

....

....

....

Three Circles

Small contributions (even to your own well-being) reverberate into the world. For visual learners, the following exercise will help you consider the effects of your micro-habits on three different levels.

The habit or practice you're choosing to keep (or release) goes at the center. The first circle represents the effect on your personal experience. The second is the effect on your family, community, or group. The third is the larger impact on your organization, culture, or society.

Fill in key words to illustrate how the change you're making reaches into each of the three domains. The outcomes that engage and excite you the most will reinforce your motivation when your energy starts to wane. To help you brainstorm, I've included an example of how Cora might fill this out based on her situation.

Cora's Three Circles
(example)

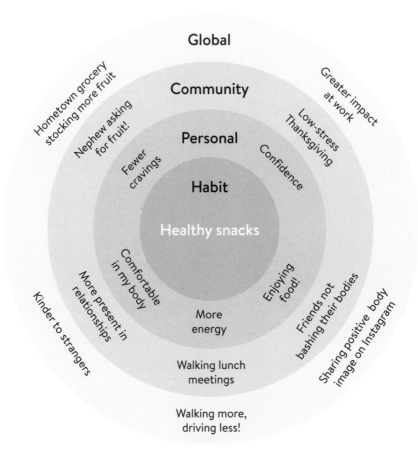

Global

Community

Personal

Habit

Healthy snacks

Hometown grocery stocking more fruit

Nephew asking for fruit!

Fewer cravings

Greater impact at work

Low-stress Thanksgiving

Confidence

Comfortable in my body

More present in relationships

Kinder to strangers

More energy

Enjoying food!

Friends not bashing their bodies

Sharing positive body image on Instagram

Walking lunch meetings

Walking more, driving less!

Three Circles

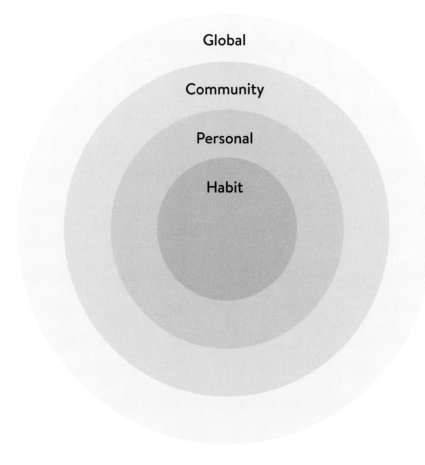

Global

Community

Personal

Habit

Elastigirl, Continued

Sifting through the rubbish in the attic, you pick up one object after another and spring back down to place them in piles on the ground outside the house. You have your trash pile and your donate pile sorted. That stuff was easy. You didn't need the nasty sheets anymore or the hand-me-down holiday lights that never worked in the first place. You didn't need the spare cushions for the wicker chair that broke back in 2004. You have boxes of books and old CDs to donate to the library, and a perfectly good hula hoop you can bring to the local elementary school.

What's left looks much less daunting. You can think clearly now. The objects from your past you have chosen to keep are purposeful. They may not all reflect exactly who you plan to be one day, but you still need them for now. They are part of you, and you're at peace with that. As you approach each remnant, you have the opportunity to determine whether it is still useful or you'd rather let it go.

Then, in a box at the back of the attic, you discover something compelling that defined you when you were younger. It's a haunting reminder of a past self that came and went, or a vision of a future self that never came to be. And there it is, the archetype of that ache, right there in the box. Maybe it represents a career path not taken. A relationship lost or endured for too long. A body that once was—or never was. You know there's no way to change the past. Even if you could go back in time, the choice wouldn't be the same as it was before. It would be different because you are different.

Do you keep this thing close or let it go? Does that aged idea still represent who you are and who you're becoming? Does the longing for it motivate you or taunt you?

This is the last thing standing between you and the stack of paint cans you were looking for in the first place. What you decide to do with it is completely your call. You can leave it in the attic for a while longer. Or you can take it down to the donation pile and clear out that bit of extra space.

Some questions to help you decide:

What is this thing? A memory, hope, goal, or identity?

....
....
....
....

What do you get out of the deal by keeping this piece of yourself?

....
....
....
....

What would you gain by letting it go?

....

....

....

....

What would you lose if you let it go?

....

....

....

....

And what would you lose by keeping it?

....

....

....

....

As usual, there are no wrong answers. All that matters is whether this thing empowers you or stifles you. Is it still part of your narrative? Is it worth keeping?

One way or the other, you make a decision to leave the thing tucked away up there or wrap your arms around it and carry it with you as you shrink back down to size—to place it gently in one of your piles: toss or give away.

On your way down, you grab your chosen paint color and set it by the front door. You found what you were looking for, but there will be time for painting later. First, you have a job to finish.

The trash fits nicely in a garbage bin outside the garage, and you're left with the donation pile. You go back inside to raise the rickety garage door. The orb is parked there next to a Ford Pinto you inherited more years ago than you can count. You don't drive it much, but now seems as good a time as any. Carefully, one at a time, you place the objects you're giving away into the car.

Loaded down, the back end of the car sags as you pull out of the driveway, grinning tooth to tail. You have taken jurisdiction, at least for today. You've determined with a clear head what you're making space for and what you no longer need. You can come back to dig deeper any time you wish, honing your truth and clearing the clutter as you go.

Breath is power, and space creates opportunity for something new and different, something chosen—on purpose.

Chapter 11

Peace

You are now entering an unfamiliar limbo zone known as *peace*. Do not be alarmed.

You dropped your donations where they belong. The house and orb are in order. The attic is clear. Distractions have abated. The absence of complications here may feel unfamiliar, perhaps even uncomfortable. Tread lightly as you seek to fill the empty space, and do not lose faith if forces beyond your control rush in to fill it like a tsunami after a category-eight earthquake.

Unburdened, you head out for a drive. The weather is fine. The skin-and-bone suit you're living in is beginning to feel more like a Porsche than a Pinto. You kick on cruise control and lean back for the first time in as long as you can remember. You're calm, with a peculiar feeling that you're capable of facing any challenge. You don't know how you'll handle what comes your way, but you know you'll manage. When you run out of gas, you'll fuel up. If a hailstorm shatters the windshield, you'll replace the glass and carry on with dents in the hood as badges of honor.

There is still work to do, of course. There is always more to do, but you're game to handle the booby traps, monkey wrenches, and a plethora of catch-22s. And between challenges, whenever you find yourself with bandwidth for change, you'll head out on the information superhighway, gathering data from your body and the world around you to figure out how those two forces jibe. You are a powerful decision-making machine. Nothing can stop you now.

The road you're on is a gentle but steady climb. You're driving toward the horizon with the sun setting before you. Up you go, and as you crest over the top of the hill—you plummet nose first into an enormous sinkhole of molasses.

Dammit! You're stuck.

You were cruising along so nicely! You had brain space and time on your hands! It felt awkward, sure, but you planned to fill it with nurturing, life-giving activities! And now this. It's not fair.

You sit in the driver's seat, considering your options. The car is slowly sinking, rear end up. The crabby, ferocious little voice in your head is back in force. *Dumbass. You didn't stand a chance of being free for long. The world is messed up, and you don't have the right to feel good. Did you actually think you could fend off the demons? Go back to beating yourself up, like old times. You're good at it. Go on now. Succumb to the molasses, or if by some miracle you make it out, you can shlump your way back home. Your old habits are waiting. Good luck getting that gooey mess off.*

Nah, you think. You're more industrious than that. You reject that bullshit outright.

Better get moving, though.

You crawl out of the driver's side window, pull yourself up on the roof, and climb over the back of the trunk. It wasn't pretty, but you made it. You stand there watching the car go down, surprised by your own strength, arms crossed, just a shade proud of yourself. The Pinto may be stuck in molasses, but you're standing on solid ground. You never really liked that thing anyway. Maybe someday you'll get your Porsche vibe on in the garage. Anyway, it was nice while it lasted.

The Goblin Spider

You set out for home on foot. The open spaces don't scare you, exactly. You know you have the agency to fill them—or leave them empty if you want. But something about all this space does feel disconcerting.

As you walk, you look down and realize there's a beastly little goblin nipping at your feet. *Seriously?* Its impish legs are scrambling to keep up as it jumps and bites at your ankles.

"Not fast enough!" it screeches with a pitiful, little rasp. "You suck!"

You kick it away, but it springs back as if tethered to you by a rubber band.

"Everything else sucks, too!" it shrieks.

SMACK. It flies off and rebounds like a giant jumping spider. Dang, that thing is persistent.

You can see the house from where you are, but out of nowhere, your legs go out from under you. The venom from all those little bites of outrage and despair makes its way into your veins, and you are lost to heartache. The weight of the world comes crashing at your feet. You sit down in the middle of the road as the Goblin Spider crawls up your back and nuzzles into the nape of your neck. You put your head between your knees to stop the world from spinning and close your eyes against the ache. It's too much—too much hate, too many assumptions and expectations, too much suffering and division.

Your mind spins. This is insane. What's the point of "habit change"?! Nothing I do makes a difference. I can't even move. How am I supposed to keep showing up for all the things—mine or anybody else's? And what's the point if I still feel this way after coming so far? I don't even know how to make it back to my body house.

You're super-adept at ignoring rational thoughts at times like this. If only you were better at ignoring your *irrational* ones. You realize this thought loop is not helpful. You know you're physically capable of getting back to the house. It isn't far, but that fact frustrates you even more. *What is wrong with me? I can do this. I should be able to get up and go. Other people have real problems, and I'm sitting around like a self-absorbed fool on a hill.*

Thankfully, you know a little something about the physiology of stress. When humans perceive stressful situations, their heart rate, blood pressure, and stress hormones go up. Muscles tense, the nervous system fires up, and digestive and immune system functions plummet.[54] You know that when you're on high alert, you are not capable of talking yourself out of these physiological responses. Your instincts take over, and your mind takes a back seat until the threat has passed. And you know from experience that if a little kid is terrified, angry, or hurt, you can't have a rational talk with them until they calm down—and adults are no different. The best you can do is hold space for them until they can breathe again.

Of course! Breath.

Jurisdiction.

You don't even have to lift your head from between your knees to take a breath, and you know you can manage that much, even with poison in your veins.

A broad-based study published in 2018 by *Frontiers in Human Neuroscience* and the National Institutes of Health reports that slow breathing techniques "increase comfort, relaxation, pleasantness, vigor and alertness, and reduce symptoms of arousal, anxiety, depression, anger, and confusion."[55] The researchers called the study "How Breath-Control Can Change Your Life: A Systematic Review on Psycho-Physiological Correlates of Slow Breathing." In academic literature, scientists don't usually claim that something "Can Change Your Life." That is the stuff of self-help gurus. But the facts are compelling enough for them to make that claim. Breathing *can* change your life. It can change your psycho-physiological life. You have big, scrappy lungs capable of changing everything.

As the venom wears off, the panic subsides. Your body begins to release, and you realize you should probably get out of the middle of the road—survival being a priority and all. You roll over to the grass median and lay down on your back. The Goblin Spider loses its grip on your neck and crawls off in search of a place to cook up some more venom.

You open your eyes to watch the clouds move in and out of view—and laugh. *It never ends, does it?* You can build all the systems you want, and feel as confident as you like about staying out of the molasses, but stress just keeps coming in one form or another: demons, goblins, a car accident, a lost job, or a lost love. The stress isn't going anywhere because this is planet Earth, and you are a mammal with a central nervous system.

But you also have some mad skills. Breathing, to start. Breath gives you the means to figure out what's next, but you're skeptical of how far this approach can take you in real life. Certainly, it's enough to get you moving, to get you walking back toward the house if you so choose, but then what? How does this have anything to do with achieving peace of mind or quality of life? Are you supposed to just sit around all day breathing? (Or *navel-gazing*, as your grandpa used to say?) What's all the buzz about mindfulness and being present with your feelings? What good does it do, and what the hell does "being present with your feelings" mean, anyway?

In his extraordinary book *The Body Keeps the Score: Brain, Mind, and Body in the Healing of Trauma*, psychiatrist, author, and researcher Bessel Van Der Kolk, MD writes, "Mindfulness not only makes it possible to survey our internal landscape with compassion and curiosity but can also actively steer us in the right direction for self-care."[56]

According to every pop psychology article you've ever read, mindfulness is how you get from messed up to functional—and from functional to productive. Everybody is always urging you to meditate when you'd rather *medicate* with sugar, salt, shopping, or something equally delicious. Meditation seems like another thing to add to your to-do list, and you don't want to "sit with your feelings." Feelings suck.

Fortunately, with all your fancy breathing skills, you don't have to "meditate" if you don't feel like it—but if one breath becomes ten, you might have to cop to involuntary meditation and reap the benefits.

When you learn how to be sad without the sadness breaking you in half, it's easier to peel yourself off the ground and get back to work—and life and play. That's the endgame with the whole breathing-meditation deal: decoupling stressful events from knee-jerk reactivity. The breath puts a sliver of light between impact and reflex.[57] It lets you practice leaning back in your Porsche while simultaneously holding on for dear life.

Peace is knowing how to unclench, come what may. It's the knowledge that, with your infrastructure in place, you possess the ability to climb out of any quagmire—no matter how dire. You can't strangle stress to death. You can try, but all that effort only increases its ferocity until it shatters your ability to contain it.

Perfection

For nearly two decades, I have observed how my clients deal with stress. I've watched venom leak into their bloodstreams in the form of oppressive jobs, toxic relationships, illnesses, loneliness, and worry. To combat the stress, some people go on the offensive: choking off their instincts and hammering away at solutions that no longer serve them. Others collapse under the weight of it: turning in on themselves and abandoning any pursuit of progress or change. Most of us swing from one extreme to the other, depending on the day. We harden our resolve for a time, striving for our "best self"—but eventually we lose momentum and settle for our present self instead. This dichotomy creates untold misery. It leaves us feeling defective when, in fact, we are anything but.

The concept of a *best self* is dubious. *Best* implies a definitive conclusion, an achievable end, but we are not static creatures. We can't achieve a state of perfection, nor should we strive to. We are spectacularly volatile, adaptable, highly attuned organisms—and what we need and want changes over time.

A fixed vision of some optimal self is inherently discouraging, and the idea that we are perpetually deficient destroys our sense of satisfaction. Even if we hit a goal, lose the weight, earn the money—there's always some other precondition required to earn that elusive status: *best self*. Rigid ideals rob us of agency and erode our health. When we refuse to bend and forget to breathe, we are too easily fractured.

Flexibility is the remedy. It's the quick fix miracle drug—and the closest we get to perfection. Being flexible allows us to put down our weapons and break free of constraints, to make space for liberty: the freedom to be okay for a bit, even in the thick of the fog.

To do that:

1. Listen: Pay attention when the signals go off.
2. Breathe: Insert space between impact and reflex.
3. Respond: Lean on your chosen coping mechanisms—some healthy, some not, but all of them *on purpose.*

Your body may not be perfect. It may even cause you pain, but there is no escaping it. It's the best resource you've got for growth and progress. As children's book author Michael Rosen wrote, "We can't go under it. We can't go over it . . . we've got to go through it."[58] No matter how dissatisfied we may be with our bodies and the habits they crave, the only way out of those patterns is through.

Circumstances are frequently beyond our control, but the ritual of coming back to our bodies provides us with precious guidance. The physical act of releasing your belly—making room for your lungs to expand, for your neck to align and hips to release—allows for the possibility of a new paradigm.

When you're in your car, cruising along at a good clip, and you drive into a sinkhole of molasses, whiplash is inevitable. But if you *don't* clamp down on the steering wheel and start screaming like an incubus with road rage—if, instead, you take a breath and roll down your window—you're a hell of a lot more likely to be able to climb out before getting sucked under. And in that knowing, there is peace.

Breath is the power to make a choice. Peace is the payoff.

The Golden Dragon

But you're not meditating now. You're just idling in the grass, watching the clouds pass by. You've got the resources you need to keep going. You're stretchy and lithe, remember? And the house is just over yonder.

With that, you sit up to find the Goblin Spider staring at you. It's dangling by one leg, in the grasp of a colossal Golden Dragon with a goofy smile.

"It belongs to you?" the Dragon says.

"Yeah, I guess it does," you say, reaching out to take the spider. It's going to keep nipping at your ankles, so you may as well keep it where you can manage it.

You place it on your shoulder, brushing it back each time it attempts to chomp down on your flesh. It's a persistent little bugger, but it's only doing its job. There's no escape, so supervision seems the better part of wisdom.

The Dragon offers to take you home, but you decline. *Wasn't this one of the creatures threatening to consume me whole if I took on too many new habits?*

"Sort of," the Dragon says, reading your mind. "Those are my cousins, but you chose the path of listening and responding. You have chosen wisely, so I can take you anywhere you want to go."

You consider this, but you've got your legs back under you now. A walk seems like a perfect way to daydream about what to do with your empty space. You'd rather walk, and, so, you do—with a Goblin Spider on your shoulder and a Golden Dragon plodding along a few steps behind.

This peaceful feeling is a little more familiar now. It's okay not to know what's next. Now that you've cleared out the clutter, take your time to muse on how far you've come and the possibilities at hand.

What was one challenging time in your past that made way for something unexpectedly wonderful?

....

....

List 3 words to describe how you felt when that stressful situation began.

....

List 3 words to describe how you felt when you moved past it.

....

How did your strengths (What You're Good At) or values (What Matters) play a part in helping you move through that situation?

....

....

....

What challenges are currently driving you to set boundaries—and how are you doing so?

....

....

....

If you have open space in your life right now, how do you want to fill or protect that space?

....

....

....

Chapter 12

Presence

When you arrive home, you part ways with the Dragon on the far side of the bridge and put the Goblin Spider on the ground, where he promptly sets about making himself a lair from which to torture you at a later date. You sit down on the front porch and pry open the paint can you left there. The color is brighter than you remember, but that's okay. You're inclined to embrace peculiarities.

You sand, scrub, and pressure wash the door, and when it's pristine and primed, you decide *Hell with it, I want a splash of color—literally.* You put the lid back on the paint, shimmy shake it until it's mixed, take the lid off again, back up a few feet, wind up, and slosh the paint over the door like a wave of heavy cream.

Giddy with the liberty of it, you kick off your shoes and step into the puddles of paint on the front porch—the color oozing between your toes. Job done, you walk around the house, leaving footprints as you go, making your way to the screened porch in the back. With vaulted ceilings, skylights, and ceiling fans, this is your favorite place on Earth. Rainstorms or sunny days, blazing heat or winter chill, this porch is your go-to when you want to be yourself.

Out here, you know exactly what wellness means. It doesn't mean perfection. It's not about striving to be completely pain-free or blissed out. Here, your body ceases being a production and becomes a conduit for living. It is the apparatus that makes everything in your life possible: work, love, pleasure, purpose, and passion. Here, you know how it feels to value your fingers and toes, heart, lungs, and all the saggy parts, just as they are. Here, you get to stop fitting into all the molds. You can just *be*. And then—free of the tit for tat in your mind—you get clear, much faster, about What Matters and what doesn't.

It's enough. It's all enough. Your body and accomplishments are enough—and you don't have to change them to be relevant and worthwhile.

The birds are singing in groups of three, perched on tree branches and power lines, chirping a happy tune. Feather-light clouds blow through a teal blue sky. You putter about pruning plants and beating pillows. You pour a drink and put your feet up, as you please.

President George W. Bush once said, "Some folks look at me and see a certain swagger, which, in Texas, is called 'walking.'"[59] On this porch, you've got swagger. You feel like a Texas oil man with Western boots, a cowboy hat, and a leathery tan—the whole rich, old white dude package. You have the absolute right to be here, and no one can tell you otherwise.

Swagger

S ay it with me now. *SWWAAAAGERRRRR.*

I love the word *swagger* like a mama cat loves her babies. I want to lick it, feed it, and nurture it until it strikes out on its own. Swagger is loose and broad, and I don't have it. Not the real kind, anyway. I have the fake version sometimes but not the grounded, exposed, irreverent kind of swagger I see in the people I most admire: Michelle Obama, Megan Rapinoe, Lizzo, Malala, Pink, Greta Thunberg. That's the kind I want.

It's not about being cocky or righteous. It's the other part of the swagger equation: the part about showing up whole—and it is my latest, chosen practice. I'm still pretty lame at it—but getting better. I've got my Wonder Woman undies on, and I'm in the orb, hanging onto my handrails, wearing combat boots, jumping out like Captain Underpants when I see people belittling their bodies and discounting their intuition. I spring up on rooftops to the soundtrack of "Le Freak" by Chic. I swing from flagpoles with a megaphone, hoping to remind folks that their bodies and minds are preposterously powerful, highly attuned machines just the way they are, and the alarm bells they hear (through aches and pains and nagging worries) are notices being dispatched from central command: *Hello? Hidy-ho! Hey there! Your troubles need tending.*

But sometimes my shoelaces get tangled in the ropes on the flagpole, and I end up hanging upside down, one foot flailing, my head turning purple as I wonder if my abs are strong enough to pull me up. And I ponder: *What right do I have to show up like this? What right do I have to put on a cape and look another human being in the eye and say, "HEY! You matter! We need you!"*

And what about you, Commando Swagger? What's your spiel? Sure, you have years of training, education, life experience, yadda, yadda. You've seen a few things. You have the qualifications. But what right do you have to do your work with impunity? What right do any of us have to be so presumptuous as to believe that the human race wants or needs what we have to offer? What gives us the authority to say, "I can help with that. I know how to do that, and I'm damn good at it"?

Halla Tómasdóttir is an Icelandic businesswoman and CEO of The B Team, a group that works internationally with purpose-driven businesses and governments to solve some of the greatest crises of our time: inequality and climate change. She also ran for president in Iceland in 2016 and came in second out of four, after raising her support in the polls from 1 percent to 29 percent in a matter of weeks.

Tómasdóttir told Guy Raz of *TED Radio Hour,* "It's a normal question to ask yourself, 'Who am I to serve?' But a better question to think about is 'Who are we not to?' If we really care and we think the world is not right . . . we need to ask ourselves, 'What am I doing?' We can't point out the window and ask other people to solve it."[60] This imperative only applies, of course, to those of us who are safe speaking out and making our voices heard. No marginalized person should be expected to solve the systemic issues sabotaging their lives.

There is space for all of us. This life is an Equal Swagger Opportunity—everybody gets to matter; everybody gets to be whole. Because the only way change happens is with at least a little swagger in your step. You have to know you're *capable* of making a different choice before you can even begin to change a habit—or build a brand or run for office. I don't care if you're trying to walk more often or solve the climate crisis, if the thing you're contributing is a part of civil society—any small part of the net that holds us all up—know that you *have a right* to show up for What Matters. And that includes your health. With even just a hint of that swagger in place, your brain can set your body in motion to stand up, put on your shoes, and do the damn thing.

I, for one, would like to know what your thing is, or what your many things are, please. I want to know who you are, What Matters, and what you want to do with that—even if it's about making fruit salad for your nephew, *especially* if it's about making fruit salad for your nephew. I want to know what you love to do, what makes time fly. And if you don't know, I hope this book helps you figure it out.

Hearing other people's stories—where their journeys have taken them and what they've figured out—keeps us connected. It's inspiring sometimes and heartbreaking sometimes, too—but we're in it together, and that makes everything better. So please, tell your story and do your thing. We need your specific part of this net to be durable. The state of the world is heavy, and the only way to sustain our collective well-being is to *listen*: to each other and to the messages coming from our own bodies.

We all have injuries and broken hearts, and we have daily bits of gravel and rain pelting our body houses, wearing them down. It's the universal plight of being alive. Some of us have been through trauma far worse than others, but we all have the same human needs and desires. And, periodically, we all find ourselves standing in pitch-dark rooms, blind and unnerved, feeling our way forward. But there's a dimmer switch, right there on the wall. If we can feel our way over to it, we can slowly nudge it up, to shed a little light, so as not to shock the system—looking for small habits, microdoses of well-being, to ease our bodies and clear our minds.

And each one, each little dose of something new, always runs through the filter of swagger. Presence.

Will this ritual open my chest? Will I listen better, to myself and to others? Will it put me in the company of people who make me feel whole? Will it alleviate worry or physical tension? Will it create space? Will it give me energy, allow me to sleep better, or reduce my pain, so I can do the things I want and build my part of the net?

Titans of industry and political leaders the world over do not have any qualms about showing up to build their empires, and many of them haven't done so well by the rest of us.

I don't know about you, but I'm about ready to get my swagger on.

365-Day Challenge

Systems make space for new habits, and new habits make space for expanded boundaries around who you are and what you're capable of. We've been playing with one of those systems here: LISTEN—BREATHE—RESPOND. Systems are critical. They offer you confidence, stability, and measurable progress, but they have limits, too. They keep you squarely in your head. Even when focused on the body, systems are cerebral. They keep you moving from box to box, shackled to your ambitions in a constant state of questioning: Am I enough? Have I gone far enough? Should I be doing more?

A friend showed me a video recently of her three-year-old daughter dancing enthusiastically in their living room. She looked at me, dead on. "I don't know how to feel like that anymore," she said. "I'm not sure I ever knew how to feel like that." She was talking about abandon. Release. An utter absence of corrosive self-consciousness. My friend wasn't longing to be unaware of herself; there's no such thing. We are all self-aware, and we should be—to make sure we interweave with the net rather than overtaking it. To have no self-awareness would be a sad state of affairs. My friend was talking about something else: what it might feel like to be *at home* in her body—free of strategies or goals—just alive and okay and here.

So I offer you a challenge. If you choose to accept it, we'll be in it together. It's one I've taken on myself.

Maybe you know what it feels like to wish you could leave your body behind on the floor of the closet with all the clothes you discarded that day, in favor of whichever outfit feels most like an invisibility cloak. Or, maybe you have avoided saying what you think in favor of someone else's opinion—someone with more power or education or money.

This is the challenge: for one year, take your body with you into every room you enter. Pin your location. It's a practice that takes, well, practice. Every "failure" along the way—every derogatory, self-deprecating comment; every unwarranted apology—is not so much a defeat as a chance to play again, to pick your body up off the floor and take it with you next time. Play it again with swagger and presence. Show up with it like Lizzo at Madison Square Garden.

I hereby commit to taking my body with me for 365 days as best I know how.

ACCEPT _____   DECLINE _____

"Beauty begins the moment you decide to be yourself."[61]

—Coco Chanel

What would be different if you showed up at a meeting or a party—whole, splendid, and less-than-perfect?

....

....

....

....

When and where you do already feel safe being whole?

....

....

....

....

Where else might you sneak in some new, incremental swagger?

....

....

....

....

The Broken Is the Beauty

The Habit Trip is a means to an end. It's a lifelong practice of treating ourselves, and others, with basic kindness and respect—radical, that. It's about learning to hear and respond to our bodies and minds, so our lives can feel better and we can help make other people's lives feel better. It's subversive shit, I tell you.

Storyteller and education advocate Sonia Fernández LeBlanc wrote in a blog post in 2017, "There's a Japanese art form and philosophy known as *Kintsukuroi* (Kint-su-ku-roy), which is a technique where broken pottery is mended with gold, silver, or platinum-dusted lacquer so that the broken piece is literally 'repaired with gold.' It's a philosophy that holds that the journey of an object's breakage and repair is an important visual of the object's history that deserves to shine through rather than be disguised. The broken is the beauty."[62]

The broken is the beauty. Destructive habits are not flaws; they're coping mechanisms that serve a purpose. They are survival techniques, protective tactics we deploy to shield us from stress, sadness, fear, grief, and frustration. They help for a minute. They really do. Otherwise, we wouldn't keep going back to them. They help, until they make us feel crummy again.

When we set a goal to make a change and then screw it up, we're usually just trying to meet a neglected need. If we can find alternative ways to fill those needs, we've got a lot better shot at leaving some of those old habits behind. Even after we've left them behind, they may pop back up again—but that's okay, too. A setback isn't a crisis. It's your body reaching for something familiar. That's all. It makes perfect sense.

To find alternatives—healthier habits that fill the void with comfort and familiarity you'll *want* to turn to for the rest of your life—you have to keep trying. You've got to stay in the game, looking under rocks and stepping through force fields, welcoming whatever unruly kerfuffle comes next.

Truth is the magic formula. All the information you need about what to do next can be found in the truth, but the truth can be hard to parse.

To gather the data you need:

1. Check with your information source (your body, instincts, partner, colleagues, or group) to hear what's working and what's not.
2. Consult with experts who have actual evidence for what has worked before (or in similar circumstances) and take their hypotheses under advisement . . . with a grain of salt.
3. Play with habits or routines to see what feels better.
4. Huddle with your people to keep vigil and celebrate new signs of life.

In the end, every decision you make is based on your best instincts, hopefully.

You are the only one who knows if it's time to stay or go, to sell or buy, to keep trying or call it quits, to pick up the cigarette or put it down, to order the lasagna or the burger. Sometimes the fries will be the best choice by a mile, but sometimes an apple with almond butter is paradise on a plate. And if you can't tell the difference, you aren't quite listening—yet.

If you listen, you can tell what's true. And if you can tell what's true, you can assess your options and make your best guess about which way to go next. We're all dosing ourselves every day—with sugar and screens, with movement, stretching, sleep, and warm batches of chocolate chip cookies. Feeling better is a matter of tipping the scales to make sure that more remedies are helping than hurting.

And if you keep moving in something-resembling-the-right-direction, one day you will look around and realize that something significant has changed. You won't be sure if it's your body or your perception, but whatever it is, it's different. And it feels awfully nice not to worry so much, to be a little nicer to yourself and everybody else, to be present and okay.

Porch Sit with Puppets

As you lean back on the porch with your feet up on the table—watching the sun set over the mountain range where you first saw the orbs knocking about—you look up and see a giant eye staring at you through the skylight.

"Hi," the Dragon says.

"How did you find me?" you ask.

"Footprints," she says. "Lonely. Go for a ride?"

"Okay, okay. We can go for a ride. Where should we go?"

"Up," she says.

You pad out of the porch, bare feet covered in paint, hair still untamed. And you climb on the Dragon's back, holding on to her scales. You feel her body sink toward the ground and then push off into the air, wings flapping gently as you rise over the house, over the treetops, higher and faster until you can smell the clouds. From there, you can see, for the first time, how small everything is—not just the house and the intersection, but the whole journey.

From this vantage point, you can see houses and intersections in every direction, lights flickering on as the sun sets behind the mountains. You can see people wandering over bridges and speeding over lakes. You can even see portals to the Liquid Brick Road glimmering from just the right angle. And orbs bouncing around, some crashing violently, others rolling with the shape of the land, and still others, parked—empty and waiting for the next seismic event.

Up here, you can see everything. You are not alone. You are part of a shared experience. Call it a mess or a miracle, but everybody else is as much a part of it as you are, no matter how different they might be from you. We're all just crashing into cliffs and trying to get back to the garage. Most of us are doing the best we can, even when we're being assholes.

Angry drunk. Oil man. Night nurse. We all need the same basic reinforcements, and we would do well to look out for each other's well-being. If everyone's orb were retrofitted with an Impact-Resistant Infrastructure Kit, the mountains would be safer for all of us to bump around like quantum particles in a popcorn machine. But a lot of folks don't know how to assemble a support system like that; or there's not enough money; or they're too exhausted, scared, or pissed off to do anything other than hang on for dear life. As it is, we're crashing into a lot of people with bumps and bruises in this cosmic popcorn machine, and exhausted people don't have time for mahogany libraries and velvet chairs. They're trying to survive when the monsters start peeking out from behind the bushes—just like you.

Breath catches in your throat as you wrap your arms around the Dragon's neck. She is euphoric—chest out, wings flapping—ecstatic to have a purpose, to have someone to lift. The two of you soar until nightfall before landing safely back at the house.

You slide off. And your ass hits the ground with a *whomp*.

"Next time! Bye-bye!" The Dragon waves gleefully and waddles off.

"Thank you," you gag, half on nitrogen and half on oxygen.

You stand and brush yourself off. You turn to go in the front door and realize that it's sealed shut with paint. *Of course*, you think. *Stupid*. It was so satisfying, though, and it's a masterpiece.

Oh well. The only way into the house, from now on, is through the porch around back, the place where your skin fits just right.

You walk through the screened door with your clothes on your body and your hair on your head. You know who you are. You know where you've been. Not sure where you're headed, but you know where to begin.

A little mischief. A little love. And a whole lot of come-what-may.

You have a caravan coming tomorrow. You've invited the cast of the Muppets, the postman and the mayor, the folks from the yarn store, the goth kids, your best friend, your senator, and your veterinarian.

You got a vet for the Goblin Spider. The little fucker keeps things interesting, and you'd never discover anything useful without him around, like how to suck venom from a wound. He did leave a nasty bite on the back of your neck, though. But you have a balm for that.

Best put something on it before it festers.

It's time for sleep. Tomorrow is another big day.

When the guests arrive, they can enter through the screened porch where there are no apologies, just succulents and snacks. And, for a special treat, maybe they'd like to see the view from above. Dragon rides for everyone. You and G. D. can take them up one by one—so they can see with their own eyes, same as you.

Do your voodoo, Commando Swagger.

365 days a year.

Further Reading

Atomic Habits: An Easy & Proven Way to Build Good Habits & Break Bad Ones, by James Clear. Avery, 2018.

The Body Keeps the Score: Brain, Mind, and Body in the Healing of Trauma, by Bessel van der Kolk, MD. Viking, 2014.

Broken Open: How Difficult Times Can Help Us Grow, by Elizabeth Lesser. Villard, 2005.

Drive: The Surprising Truth About What Motivates Us, by Daniel H. Pink. Riverhead Books, 2011.

Joy on Demand: The Art of Discovering the Happiness Within, by Chade-Meng Tan. Harper One, 2016.

The Mindful Diet: How to Transform Your Relationship with Food for Lasting Weight Loss and Vibrant Health, by Ruth Q. Wolever, PhD, and Beth Reardon, MS, RD, LDN, with Tania Hannan. Scribner, 2015.

My Grandmother's Hands: Racialized Trauma and the Pathway to Mending Our Hearts and Bodies, by Resmaa Menakem. Central Recovery Press, 2017.

No Sweat: How the Simple Science of Motivation Can Bring You a Lifetime of Fitness, by Michelle Segar, PhD. AMACOM, 2015.

The Power of Habit: Why We Do What We Do in Life and Business, by Charles Duhigg.Random House. 2012.

Stumbling on Happiness, by Daniel Gilbert. Vintage, 2007.

Tiny Habits: The Small Changes that Change Everything, by BJ Fogg, PhD. Houghton Mifflin Harcourt, 2019.

The Willpower Instinct: How Self-Control Works, Why It Matters, and What You Can Do to Get More of It, by Kelly McGonigal, PhD. Avery, 2011.

Acknowledgments

Ken, you keep the beat when I have lost all sense of time and place. The orb came calling for us by the end of this process, and you showed up with a backhoe to clear the way. You are the kindest, most generous and creative person I know, and I am so grateful to be on this road with you.

Sky, thank you for teaching me about dragons and spiders and superheroes. You are the inspiration for this story, through and through. I hope you like it because it likes you.

Moon, despite your many attempts to type, I believe I have successfully deleted your line edits. You are a hot mess, but you showed up just in time to remind me how important ritual is—that a routine, no matter how small, can make or break a day.

Ringo, you are my Golden Dragon. Your gentle spirit always brings me home no matter how far I stray.

To my family, thank you for leaving me in London at age seventeen with a copy of *The Bell Jar*—and trusting me to find my way back.

Jana, you give me a foam pit full of rainbows in which to land—without fail, every time. You are the platform beneath my feet, and I love you more than you will ever know.

Julia, I didn't realize that jigsaw puzzles could heal the gaping chasms of the soul, but at your house, I learned that they can. You're wise like a mama owl, and I'm just trying to keep up. Thank you for your vision.

Tracy, I left my water bottle in your van. Next time you're stateside, I'll meet you in a field by a freeway with a blanket and a bag of chips. You can tell me about spinal fluid and where to find the wind. Maybe someday we'll figure out why it matters—and why it doesn't.

Mayo Clinic faculty and students, you are building a floor that all of us can stand on. I am so grateful for this growing community of caregivers. My time there this past year was sheer bliss, except for that one day.

Thank you, Stacey, for taking this leap with me, and Jac, for bringing me back into the fold and peppering my world with provocative, awe-inspiring things to look at.

To Kristen and the team at Running Press, thank you for making books that feel like works of art, for stretching with me and pushing me off various cliffs. I'm nothing if not game. You made this book more beautiful and accessible than I ever imagined it could be.

And most of all, to my clients, thank you for letting me be part of your journeys, for showing me how every path is both achingly familiar and wildly unique. You amaze and inspire me by always landing on your feet, even when you've taken a beastly tumble. You remind me that, with a little support, I can bounce back, too. We all can. Hearing your stories reinforces, every day, that if we're listening, we always know what to do next.

Endnotes

1   Salman Rushdie, "One Thousand Days" (speech, Columbia University, December 11, 1991, archived by WNYC), https://www.wnyc.org/story/239518-one-thousand-days-salman-rushdie-columbia-1991/.

2   Dolly Parton (@DollyParton), "Find out who you are and do it on purpose," Twitter, April 8, 2015, 3:40 p.m., https://twitter.com/dollyparton/status/585890099583397888.

3   This is how Glinda, the Good Witch, from the film *The Wizard of Oz* is commonly misquoted. The actual line in the script reads, "You've always had the power to go back to Kansas."

4   Thor Hanso, "What is Orbing and Is It Safe?", EzineArticles.com, November 9, 2009, http://EzineArticles.com/3238493.

5   The most widely known commercial brand for orbing is ZORB, based in Rotorua, New Zealand. https://zorb.com/.

6   Joseph Campbell, *The Hero with a Thousand Faces* (Pantheon Books, 1949).

7   Annabel Acton, "How to Set Goals (and Why You Should Write Them Down)," *Forbes*, November 3, 2017, https://www.forbes.com/sites/annabelacton/2017/11/03/how-to-set-goals-and-why-you-should-do-it/#90c520b162d3.

8   Chade-Meng Tan, *Joy on Demand: The Art of Discovering Happiness Within* (Harper One, 2016).

9   Patrick Finan, PhD, "The Effects of Sleep Deprivation," infographic, Johns Hopkins Medicine, https://www.hopkinsmedicine.org/health/wellness-and-prevention/the-effects-of-sleep-deprivation.

10   Bryan Lufkin, "Does an Extra Hour of Sleep Matter?", BBC.com, January 4, 2019, https://www.bbc.com/worklife/article/20190104-does-an-extra-hour-of-sleep-matter.

11   Heidi Godman, "Regular Exercise Changes the Brain to Improve Memory, Thinking Skills," *Harvard Health Letter*, April 9, 2014, https://www.health.harvard.edu/blog/regular-exercise-changes-brain-improve-memory-thinking-skills-201404097110.

12   Meg Selig, "Is It True That 'Movement Is Medicine'?", *Psychology Today*, March 30, 2017, https://www.psychologytoday.com/us/blog/changepower/201703/is-it-true-movement-is-medicine.

13   "Exercise: 15 Minutes a Day Ups Lifespan by 3 Years," *Harvard Heart Letter*, December 2013, https://www.health.harvard.edu/heart-health/exercise-15-minutes-a-day-ups-lifespan-by-3-years.

14   Council on School Health, "The Crucial Role of Recess in School," *Pediatrics* (January 2013), 131 (1) 183–188; https://doi.org/10.1542/peds.2012-2993.

15   Marco Iacoboni, "The Mirror Neuron Revolution: Explaining What Makes Humans Social," interview by Jonah Lehrer, *Scientific American*, July 1, 2008, https://www.scientificamerican.com/article/the-mirror-neuron-revolut/.

16   Amy Novotney, "Social Isolation: It Could Kill You," American Psychological Association, May 2019, https://www.apa.org/monitor/2019/05/ce-corner-isolation.

17   Jamie Ducharme, "This Is the Amount of Money You Need to Be Happy, According to Research," Money, February 14, 2018, http://money.com/money/5157625/ideal-income-study/.

18   Y. Wang, B. F. Jones, & D. Wang, "Early-Career Setback and Future Career Impact." *Nature Communications* 10, 4331 (2019), https://doi.org/10.1038/s41467-019-12189-3.

19   Yuki Noguchi, "Creative Recruiting Helps Rural Hospitals Overcome Doctor Shortages," NPR.org, August 8, 2019, https://www.npr.org/sections/health-shots/2019/08/15/747023263/creative-recruiting-helps-rural-hospitals-overcome-doctor-shortages.

20   This client's name and identifying details have been changed to protect her privacy.

21   Henri J. M. Nouwen, *Bread for the Journey* (Harper One, 2006).

22   Green Linnet, https://www.greenlinnets.com/.

23   Credit for this quote, of course, goes to Monopoly by Hasbro. https://monopoly.hasbro.com/en-us.

24   Daniel Gilbert, *Stumbling on Happiness* (Vintage, 2007).

25   Michelle Obama, *Becoming* (Crown Publishing Group, 2018).

26   "You vs. Future You; or Why We're Bad at Predicting Our Own Happiness," *Hidden Brain*. NPR, August 23, 2016, https://www.npr.org/2016/08/23/490972873/you-vs-future-you-or-why-were-bad-at-predicting-our-own-happiness.

27   Screenplay by Jennifer Lee, *Frozen II*, Walt Disney Pictures, 2019.

28   "Life Expectancy," World Health Organization, Global Health Observatory Data, 2000–2016, https://www.who.int/gho/mortality_burden_disease/life_tables/situation_trends_text/en/.

29   Louis Newman, "The Refreshing Practice of Repentance," *On Being with Krista Tippett*, podcast, September 17, 2014, https://onbeing.org/programs/louis-newman-the-refreshing-practice-of-repentance/.

30   "The Ideal Temperature for Sleep," Sleep.org, https://www.sleep.org/articles/temperature-for-sleep/.

31   "Volunteering and Its Surprising Benefits," Helpguide.org, https://www.helpguide.org/articles/healthy-living/volunteering-and-its-surprising-benefits.htm.

32   Kelly McGonigal, *The Willpower Instinct: How Self-Control Works, Why It Matters, and What You Can Do To Get More of It* (Avery, 2011).

33   Charles Duhigg, *The Power of Habit: Why We Do What We Do in Life and Business* (Random House, 2012).

34   Craig Bloem, "Why Successful People Wear the Same Thing Every Day," Inc, 2018, https://www.inc.com/craig-bloem/this-1-unusual-habit-helped-make-mark-zuckerberg-steve-jobs-dr-dre-successful.html.

35   James Clear, Atomic Habits: An Easy & Proven Way to Build Good Habits & Break Bad Ones (Avery, 2018).

36   Cathryn Delude, "Brain Researchers Explain Why Old Habits Die Hard," MIT News, October 19, 2005, http://news.mit.edu/2005/habit.

37   David DiSalvo, "Could We One Day Switch Off Bad Habits in Our Brains?", *Forbes*, October 31, 2012, https://www.forbes.com/sites/daviddisalvo/2012/10/31/study-suggests-that-well-one-day-be-able-to-switch-off-bad-habits-in-our-brains/#37531e971779.

38   73 magazine, March 1967, http://www.arimi.it/wp-content/73/03_March_1967.pdf.

39   The Oxford English Dictionary definition of "scientific method," referenced by Simple English Wikipedia, https://simple.wikipedia.org/wiki/Scientific_method.

40   Kaitlin Woolley and Ayelet Fishbach, "Immediate Rewards Predict Adherence to Long-Term Goals," *Personality and Social Psychology Bulletin*, 2016, https://faculty.chicagobooth.edu/ayelet.fishbach/ research/Woolley&FishbachPSPB.pdf.

41   "Reasoning in Science," Biology4kids.com, http://www.biology4kids.com/files/studies_scimethod.html.

42   Benjamin Gardner, Phillippa Lally, and Jane Wardle, "Making Health Habitual: The Psychology of 'Habit-formation' and General Practice," *British Journal of General Practice* (2012 Dec), 62(605): 664–666, accessed via US National Library of Medicine, National Institutes of Health, https://www.ncbi.nlm.nih. gov/pmc/articles/PMC3505409/.

43   Marie Kondo, *The Life Changing Magic of Tidying Up: The Japanese Art of Decluttering and Organizing* (Ten Speed Press, 2014).

44   Marcia Masulla, Roar Nashville, https://www.roarnashville.com/.

45   David Gelles, "At Aetna, a C.E.O.'s Management by Mantra," *New York Times*, February 27, 2015, https://www.nytimes.com/2015/03/01/business/at-aetna-a-ceos-management-by-mantra.html.

46   R Wolever, KJ Bobinet, K. McCabe, ER Mackenzie, E. Fekete, CA Kusnick, & M. Baime, M. "Effective and Viable Mind-body Stress Reduction in the Workplace: A Randomized Controlled Trial," *Journal of Occupational Health Psychology* (2012), 17, (2), 246–258. https://doi.org/10.1037/a0027278.

47   Cale D. Magnuson and Lynn A. Barnett, "The Playful Advantage: How Playfulness Enhances Coping with Stress," *Leisure Sciences* (2013), 35:2, 129–144, https://doi.org/10.1080/01490400.2013.761905.

48   NF Gordon, RD Salmon, BS Wright, GC Faircloth, KS Reid, TL Gordon. "Clinical Effectiveness of Lifestyle Health Coaching: Case Study of an Evidence-Based Program," *Am J Lifestyle Med.* (2016), 11(2), 153–166, https://doi.org/10.1177/1559827615592351.

49   Math Janssen, Yvonne Heerkens, Witske Kuijer, Beatrice van der Heijden, Josephine Engels, "Effects of Mindfulness-based Stress Reduction on Employees' Mental Health: A Systematic Review," *PLOS ONE* (January 24, 2018), https://doi.org/10.1371/journal.pone.0191332.

50   Mark R. Rosekind, PhD, Kevin B. Gregory, BS, Melissa M. Mallis, PhD, Summer L. Brandt, MA, Brian Seal, PhD, and Debra Lerner, PhD, "The Cost of Poor Sleep: Workplace Productivity Loss and Associated Costs," *Journal of Occupational and Environmental Medicine*, vol. 52, no. 1 (January 2010), 91–98, https://pdfs.semanticscholar.org/ce42/7217e0dcf2e47b5af717ef4f2b986ee0f90b.pdf.

51   Kristine Wong, "There's No Price Tag on a Clear Mind: Intel to Launch Mindfulness program," *Guardian*, 2014, https://www.theguardian.com/sustainable-business/price-intel-mindfulness-program-employee.

52   Toni Morrison, "The Truest Eye," interview with Pam Houston, *O, The Oprah Magazine*, November 2003, https://www.oprah.com/omagazine/toni-morrison-talks-love/all.

53   This client's name and identifying details have been changed to protect her privacy.

54   Kelsey Graham, "The Physiology of Stress and How to Manage It," ACE: American Council on Exercise, April 25, 2019, https://www.acefitness.org/education-and-resources/lifestyle/blog/7278/the-physiology-of-stress-and-how-to-manage-it.

55   A. Zaccaro, A. Piarulli, M. Laurino, E. Garbella, D. Menicucci, B. Neri, and A. Gemignani, "How Breath-Control Can Change Your Life: A Systematic Review on Psycho-Physiological Correlates of Slow Breathing," *Frontiers in Human Neuroscience* (2018), 12: 353, https://doi.org/10.3389/fnhum.2018.00353.

56   Bessell Van der Kolk, MD, *The Body Keeps the Score: Brain, Mind, and Body in the Healing of Trauma* (Penguin, 2015).

57   There is a beautiful quote often attributed to Viktor Frankl that runs very much along the lines of this idea. He is purported to have said, "Between stimulus and response there is a space. In that space is our power to choose our response. In our response lies our growth and our freedom." The source of this quote remains unclear and there are various versions floating about, but, whoever said or adapted it, it remains one of the truest things ever written. https://quoteinvestigator.com/2018/02/18/response/.

58   Michael Rosen (author) and Helen Oxenbury (illustrator), *We're Going On A Bear Hunt* (Walker Books, 1989).

59   George W. Bush, "President's Remarks at the 2004 Republican National Convention," White House Archives, September 2, 2004. https://georgewbush-whitehouse.archives.gov/news/releases/2004/09/20040902-2.html.

60   Halla Tómasdóttir, "How Can Leaders Inspire Others to Lead?", *TED Radio Hour*, NPR, May 18, 2018, https://www.npr.org/2018/05/18/612159658/halla-t-masd-ttir-how-can-leaders-inspire-others-to-lead.

61   This quote is widely attributed to Coco Chanel, but the specific reference is unknown.

62   Sonia Fernandez LeBlank, https://revolutions.me/2019/09/23/flames-through-the-broken/.

INDEX

accumulation of stuff, 159

Additional Habits, 129–130, 136–139

adulthood, early, 59

Aetna, 159

American Academy of Pediatrics, 24

American Journal for Lifestyle Medicine, 159

American Psychological Association, 27

armor, 156–158

art, as reinforcement, 146–149

assumptions, build-up of, 4

Atomic Habits (Clear), 126

autonomy, 44, 46–48

B Team, The, 186

baseline, 52–53

Becoming (Obama), 78–79

best self, concept of, 178

Biology 4 Kids, 130

Body Keeps the Score, The (Van Der Kolk), 177

brain fog, exercise and, 20

Brain Mapping Center (UCLA), 26

brainstorming, 83–85

Bread for the Journey (Nouwen), 51

breath, 159–160, 176–177, 178–179

British Journal of General Practice, 135

broken is the beauty, 190–191

Bush, George W., 184

Campbell, Joseph, 7

Chanel, Coco, 189

change
 intrinsically driven behavioral, xiii–xiv
 taking first steps toward, 89–93

circadian rhythms, 16

Clear, James, 126

clutter, purging, 153–155, 168–171

connection, 49–50

Council on School Health, 24

Crushing It Skill Set, 61

cues, 126–127, 135

denial, 44–45, 49–50

Dr. Dre, 126

Duhigg, Charles, 125–127, 129

early adulthood, 59

early-career setbacks, impact of, 36–37

eating disorder example, 46–48

Edison, Thomas, 127

"Effects of Mindfulness-Based Stress Reduction on Employees' Mental Health," 159–160

Emergency Plan, 145–149

emoji volcano, 74

environment. *See* space

exercise, 20–21

expertise, 49–50

failure, 36–37, 161

favorite things
 identifying, 72–73
 micro- and macro-versions of, 74–75
 Town of, 67–75, 147

fear of unknown, 81–82

Finan, Patrick, 16

fitness, 20–21, 48, 102–104

flexibility
 as remedy, 178
 workplace, 160

food
 as area of well-being, 18–19
 assessment of, 99–101
 as reinforcement, 146–149

Forbes, 8

Frontiers in Human Neuroscience, 176

future
 brainstorming about, 83–85
 reflection on, 77–85

Gallup World Poll, 28

Gilbert, Daniel, 78, 79

goal setting, 123–143

Goblin Spider, 175–177, 180

Golden Dragon, 180–181, 192–193

Gospel of Positive Reinforcement, 68–69

groundedness, 84

Guardian, 160

NOTES: